GW00708260

WATCHING THE WORLD

WATCHING THE WORLD

by

Jeff Jenkins

ARTHUR H. STOCKWELL LTD
Torrs Park, Ilfracombe, Devon, EX34 8BA
Established 1898
www.ahstockwell.co.uk

ISBN 978-0-7223-4227-5
Printed in Great Britain by
Arthur H. Stockwell Ltd
Torrs Park   Ilfracombe
Devon EX34 8BA

Foreword

The day came when I could stand it no longer! Whenever I arrived anywhere (usually with a burst of "You're not gonna believe this. . . .") the people around me knew they would be in for yet another tale of woe about something that had just happened to me during my journey. Some would look at me blankly, others with a look of semi-despair and a shake of the head. There were also those who would look at me and state with some authority, "I don't know why you don't write all this down." My answer was always that no one would believe me, but then finally I thought, 'It's no good – I *will* have to write it down.'

This got me concentrating on what was happening all around me. From walking to the local Co-op to flying to Sydney, as far as I was concerned everyone was fair game; and now the time has come to put you all together in one neat little volume, and here you all are.

I know that there are a huge number of people-watchers out there – and to an extent we all are, aren't we? Well, let me put it this way: if someone tells us that the moon is 268,000 miles away, then we believe it, but put a 'WET PAINT' sign on a bench and within ten minutes someone will walk past and touch it with their finger to make sure that it is! Watch them – they will. Still not convinced? Well, next time someone asks you the time, watch not how they say it, but how they do it. The index finger of one hand will always be pointed at or tapped on the back of the wrist of the other arm.

Now, I don't know if you are going to believe what you are about to read or not, but I can assure you that some, most or indeed all the events related in this book have happened (or will happen) to you at some point; and I wish you the very best of luck in trying not to laugh when they do!

So if you are ready, dear readers and fellow watchers, take a deep breath, plunge headlong into this book and read all about yourselves. See for yourself what you spend your time getting up to, and rest assured that there is someone not a million miles away from you watching you do it and noting it all down for posterity.

Now it's 'thank-you time'. A great big thank you must go to all those people who have sometimes accompanied me on my 'world-watching' trips. To be fair, most of them probably didn't even know, at the time, that there I was keeping an eye on the surrounding masses as a future subject for a book, but their company was appreciated just the same. And last, but by absolutely no means least, a huge thank you to the aforementioned surrounding masses, without whom this book would never have happened. Yes – that's you!

Jeff Jenkins

Chapter 1

Love Me, Love My Dog

I am utterly convinced that one of the world's stupidest and most useless inventions is the extending dog lead. I cannot imagine what was going through the mind of whoever invented it, and I don't understand why anyone wants to buy it!

As a kid growing up, to me, a dog with a human came in two different ways: either attached to the dog walker on your common or garden dog lead or with the pooch unrestrained. This marvellous 'third way' invention was unknown.

We, the public who are dogless, now have to contend with a dog coming towards us and its owner being attached somewhere up to twenty yards apart (OK, that might be a tad exaggerated). If this is a head-on approach, this will result in the dog going one way and the increasingly distant owner going the other with an immensely huge tripwire in between. Usually, this results in the casual pedestrian standing still until the entire ensemble has shuffled past. If, however, you arrive side on with dog to your left, owner to your right and tripwire stretched out between, you have nowhere to go. One particular owner never batted an eyelid when I casually stepped over the six-inches-off-the-ground washing line that confronted me. This was my Plan C. Plan A was to limbo underneath it; Plan B to Fosbury-flop over it! I think the greatest extending-dog-lead show I have ever seen has to be the woman with two leads, one in each hand, both fully extended. One dog was twenty feet behind her and one was twenty feet in front of her. The whole circus was longer than a double-decker bus!

Almost everything in our lives now has 'Health & Safety' stamped all over it, so for the life of me why doesn't the extending dog lead come with a government health warning? At the very least, there should be a day's course, at the end of which the proud owner is presented with an Extending Dog Lead Handler's Certificate. Dog owners must have their certificate on their person at all times when in possession of an extending dog lead – with or without a canine attached to it.

For the life of me I do not understand why dog owners don't shorten the lead when someone walks past, instead of letting it run out. If they don't reel it in, why not just have the mutt run off the lead? Better still, how about banning the thing altogether and going back to bog-standard conventional dog-walking? Then we could have ceremonial extending-dog-lead burnings up and down the country. I would be only too happy to get this under way with several litres of petrol and a box of Swan Vestas.

This brings me to another dog-related issue – one that exists with either a conventional dog lead or the dreaded extending one. If you ask any doggie walker if they say "C'mon," they will deny it on the life of a relative. Why, as soon as any dog is taken off a lead and then runs off to do anything that its doggie heart desires, does the owner always turn round and say, "C'mon," in the same squeaky off-key high-pitched voice? It doesn't matter if the owner is short, tall, male, female, nine or ninety they *all* do it, and they will *all* deny it. They will!

I have even taken a walk with a lady friend, and she was doing an elderly relative a favour by walking her dog at the same time. I felt the urge to pop the question to her (no not that one). I asked why all dog walkers say, "C'mon," in the same voice. Her vehement denial had to be heard to be believed. I was told in absolutely no uncertain terms that she never, never, never said that! I tell you, readers, we hadn't gone fifty yards when we came to a busy road, and, without being asked, the dog

8

diligently sat down and waited. As soon as a gap in the traffic appeared, guess what? Yep – she glanced down at the dog, and the same word spoken in the same way came out of her mouth: "C'mon." Then she exclaimed, "Oh, my God!" three times, and the look of utter disbelief on her face as she looked at me said it all. I hasten to add that the smug and all-knowing look on my face said it all too.

The last head-shakingly unbelievable thing that I have seen with regard to this subject is a gent walking his dog, stopping, turning and saying, "C'mon," to his pooch, which was lagging about thirty feet behind. The best bit: it was attached to an extending dog lead. I mean, why didn't he just reel it in, like a fish? A dogfish! Ha ha, d'ya geddit?

Another great subject for denials is doggie-poop collecting. Dog owners always insist that they pick up after their dogs, and I'm sure many of you out there never miss a single piece (hope you're not eating, readers, whilst reading this), but the claim that "I always pick it up" from all doggie owners just isn't true. Yet another squelch on the pavement and a look-down at your shoe confirms this to not be the case.

However (sorry – I'm not done with this if you're still eating), there's more! Many of those good citizens out there that do always pick up after their dog go about it in the most curious and furtive way imaginable when there's collecting to be done. The totally organised collector will have their box of doggie-poop bags at the ready. (Do they actually sell these?) The less well organised will have a stock of those small plastic bags that you get from the meat counter of most major supermarkets. The collection process is always the same: turn bag inside out over hand, grab poop, turn bag right way round over poop and dispose of. But why is the process so often carried out furtively? It is as if the poo collector has found a bundle of fivers and is trying to pick them up and smuggle them away without arousing any suspicion of the unsuspected windfall.

In some places there are specially placed doggie-poop bins, though, like policemen, there is never one around when you want

9

one. Now, I'm not saying that there aren't those that actually put it in an ordinary street litter bin, or even those who take it home and put it in their own bin (at least I hope that's what they do with it when they take it home), but in my experience a general walk that crosses any recognised well-used dog-walking route will always present you with a little (usually blue, though sometimes white) bag hanging from a branch of a large bush or a small tree.

(I'm sorry if your food has gone cold, but hopefully you can reheat it. I'm done now on this subject.)

I don't want you to get the impression that I don't like dogs. That is not the case at all. I always watch *One Man and His Dog*, and I have had several flutters (and won) on the dogs on many occasions, but the fact remains that we, erm, don't really get on and never have. Any other animal on the planet is fine, but dogs and I have never hit it off. I have actually turned down the advances of a possible female suitor purely on the basis that she owned a dog. People say to me, "You mustn't show that you're afraid." I'm not – no, really I'm not. 'Absolutely terrified' I've always found to be more appropriate! The next piece of advice is "Don't run." Run? How is that going to happen when I'm standing there rooted to the spot like an Antony Gormley statue! And then there's the other classic: "Oh, he only wants to play." This statement issues forth from all dog owners as your arm vanishes up to your elbow in the mouth of their adorable(!) pet dachshund (or should that be Rottweiler?) No matter. What's the difference? They all carry the wolf gene and see me as a potential aperitif.

Still not convinced? I was on a beach, minding my own business, for a change – when this big brown hound stopped dead in its tracks and looked at me. The couple supposedly walking it looked totally aghast and utterly astounded at Alice(!) as she snarled and bared her teeth at me – that's the dog not the woman.

"I am terribly sorry," said Mrs Woman. "She's never done that before."

Well, she did it when she saw me!

The man also uttered an embarrassed "Sorry."

Stupid bitch – that's the dog not the woman – oh, I don't know, though.

I know that I'm not imagining it. If I'm somewhere and an owner lets their pooch off its lead, it matters not how many other people are in the vicinity; it is me that it earmarks for its next potential meal. It then makes a direct beeline for wherever I am. It then yaps at me, watching me grow paler and my hair turn whiter. And what do I get from this savage beast's keeper, sited 100 yards away? "Oh, he only wants to play." Do you know, I think this all stems from being made to watch *The Hound of the Baskervilles* as a child, but Basil Rathbone has yet to appear to prise the monster hound off me.

In some areas of our green and pleasant land we have what are laughably known as dog wardens. Trust me, readers, this is also a subject that I would like to talk to you about in this chapter, but I feel I am unable to do so because for the life of me I have absolutely no idea what it is that these people do. Even if one sat me down and told me in infinite detail all their job entails, I can assure you that I have never seen them doing whatever it is they do in the area where I live.

I titled this chapter 'Love Me, Love My Dog', and in none of the theatres of life is this saying more appropriate than on public transport. Is there anyone out there who can possibly explain to me why it is that if a passenger gets on to a bus with a dog, no matter how scruffy a mutt the animal might be, this dog suddenly becomes the centre of the universe? No generation is untouched; all ages feel the absolute need to go "Ahhh!" or "Isn't he lovely!" Some go as far as patting and stroking the thing, and some even go as far as flinging their arms round its neck as if it was a soldier returning from the front! The owner has clearly seen all this before and sits there quite happily whilst this adoration is bestowed upon their beloved pooch, and is then ready for any question that is fired at them.

"How old is he?"

"How long have you had him?"

"Where are you taking him now?"

The list, readers, goes on and on, and every time the owner comes back with the answer quicker than if they were sitting in the black chair on *Mastermind.*

"Your name, please?"

"A. N. Other Dog Owner."

"Occupation?"

"Doggie-woggie handler."

"And your specialist subject?"

"My mutt."

"You have two minutes . . ." etc., etc.

It doesn't stop with them getting off the bus either. Within thirty seconds of the dog's departure we then have a murmur of "Wasn't he nice? Wasn't he lovely? I've always liked those sort o' dogs. My neighbour had one, you know. What breed did you say it is again? I'd like a dog, but my doctor says I can't have one – not with my knee."

Dogs and buses do tend to go together. Although I've had less experience of dogs on trains, one instance stands out above all others. The train in question was leaving London Paddington on its way to the West Country and I was sitting in a first-class carriage. The two seats opposite me, on the other side of the table, were empty as the train pulled out. At Reading a middle-aged gentleman entrained. He was dressed a little like a university lecturer, shall we say? He held a small case in one hand and a dog lead in the other. The other end of the lead was attached to a somewhat scruffy mutt. He walked down the carriage looking at the labels on the top of the seats and constantly checking them with the ticket he had in his hand. Can you guess, dear readers, which two seats he was looking for? Yep – correct! That's *two* seats – one for him and one for the scruff hound – first class! The dog took one look at me and I swear its eyes glazed over. It didn't need a menu – it knew what it was going to eat: *me!*

What happened next was akin to winning the lottery. Professor

Scruff looked at me through his floppy fringe and over his pince-nez and said, "I hope you like dogs."

I noted that this wasn't a question; it was a statement.

Somehow, in a split second, I gathered every inch of resolve and said in a low but firm voice, in an absolute masterpiece of understatement, "Er, no, not really, I don't."

"Oh," he said.

He stopped dead in his tracks and while his mutt salivated at me he came up with a solution.

"Oh," he said again quite suddenly.

In one movement his wax jacket was collected from the rack, case picked up and dog tugged off the seat and he went off muttering, to find a seat elsewhere down the carriage. He managed to find two other seats next to an elderly lady, who (I am guessing) was asked the same question as me and stumbled over her answer.

All I could think of was that I had survived the greatest threat to my life that I had ever had – and where was my Victoria Cross?

Why do people cuddle dogs they don't know? I was sitting on a bench catching some sun, one day in late summer, when a fairly tall woman in her twenties with an enormous Dobermann sat on an adjacent bench. After she had spent about five minutes doing her make-up (yes, really) whilst holding the dog lead in her hand, a bloke aged about sixty suddenly spotted the dog. At his arrival he was just a normal, regular guy; however, over the next ten seconds he promptly regressed to a child of five. He started making gibbering and cooing noises at the dog and then proceeded to walk over and pat it on its head, then its flanks; and then he tickled it under its chin. Finally he ended up on his knees stroking it all over whilst the dippy Dobermann slurped his face! Less than five minutes later it was all over; everything was as it was before. The woman continued with her mascara, and the man carried on walking to wherever it was he was going. The only thing that had really changed was the expression on my face, which had gone from relaxed serenity to total bewilderment.

All right, readers, I know I'm on my own with this (well, not totally), but I do accept that we British are a nation of dog lovers over all other pets. But come on (or should that be 'c'mon'?) – you have to admit that a person with a pooch stands apart from the rest of us. For me, they stand alone in a world of watching as being the best subject and biggest inspiration to sit down and write this book. Oh, doggie people, I thank you. Please don't ever change – you're the best!

Chapter 2

Transports of Delight, Part 1:
The Wheels on the Bus Go Round and Round

To my mind there is a very strong school of thought and also it has to be said that the best thing you can really do is to pretend to be asleep. However, this doesn't always work; you tend to nod off and then you come round to find that you have either been snoring your head off or (worse) been dribbling down your tie. I'm referring, of course, to all those thousands of bus and train journeys that a confirmed pedestrian, like me, has taken and the myriad of quite unbelievable events ranging from the utterly strange and the positively weird all the way through to the bizarre, and ending at the idontbelievethatreallyhappened.com.

I was only days old when my mother first took me on a bus, and she continued to do this until I reached the age of seven. I only have hazy memories of this time, but I remember that there was always something comforting about the old buses with the conductor coming down the bus and issuing you with a 'proper' ticket.

There were then a few years when I didn't need to catch a bus as we had a family car, but when I was eleven the need was there again. I passed my eleven-plus, which meant that my school was going to be ten miles from where I lived, and this necessitated a bus journey (or two) to get me to and from. The school bus journey home was pure joy and invariably the highlight of the day. A mishmash of kids from different schools all travelled home together, and we all showed the signs of battle of another day of what they laughingly called state education. Also, I met my first serious girlfriend on the bus home, and I would occasionally get to play cards with my best mate – not poker or brag, we were too advanced for that. Nah, it was always best-of-three games of beat your neighbour. This was the only game that we could both agree on the rules, and, trust me, we had some real humdingers of games!

The time came and I had to leave school and the bus journey behind and find alternative ways to get to work; but, as chance would have it, in my late twenties the opportunity came again to travel the same route I had taken as a spotty youth – a route that I was then to take five days a week for the next sixteen years, and the bulk of my experience of 'bussy' events comes from this era.

Standing and waiting for a bus can be one of the most comical or excruciating things you can watch. Very few people can ever manage to stand still whilst waiting for a bus at a bus stop. They wander about or hop from foot to foot in anticipation like some kind of tribal dance. The timetable is the biggest cause of this, I've noticed. If a timetable is posted up at a bus stop and a non-regular arrives to check it, I can guarantee that they will check it again when the bus arrival time has arrived and the bus hasn't. Two minutes later they will check it again, and again five minutes later. They will then seek out a fellow intending passenger (and I bet you can guess, dear readers, who that will be) with an "Excuse me. Do you have any idea when the next bus is due?" Yes, this really happens. As the expression goes, if I'd had a fiver for every time it happened, I wouldn't be sitting here writing this. Unfortunately I tend to get sarky at this point, because I'm probably hacked off that the bus hasn't turned up too.

"What does the timetable say?" is my usual reply.

And then, guess what happens next? They only walk over and check it again and come back with "It should be here now" or "Is it normally this late?"

Somehow I find myself defending the bus company at this point, perhaps because I am a regular traveller and haven't just popped along for a one-off because the car is being serviced or the wife wants it today.

"No, no, it's usually pretty good," I say, all-knowing, and the conversation then ends because the late-running bus lurches round the corner.

What happens next I can excuse the occasional bus traveller for, but never a regular. The bus has stopped and the doors are open. The person that gets on first has been catching the bus for years and they know to pay when they get on, so how come they have no money in their hand to pay for their ticket? They must have known they were about to get on a bus – after all, they've only been standing there for twenty minutes! The alternative is the regular who does have the money in their hand, only it's a £20 note for a journey which they know costs only £3.80. They know the driver has rarely got any change and certainly never that much. They catch the bus every day. How do they have the nerve to do this?

Sorry, folks – I needed to get this one off my chest. 'Tis one of my bugbears of life!

So we're on the bus, we've found our seat and we can look forward to being driven to work and having twenty-five minutes relaxation before enduring another day at the coalface. Oh, no! At the very next stop after mine a woman aged in her late fifties used to get on, and at the very next stop after that her friend/ work colleague would get on. We were then subjected to the most inane and banal chattering I have ever experienced in all my years of bus travel. Granted, this only went on for eighteen months until woman one (that's Iris, by the way) retired, but every day it was annoying to the point where I was wondering whether if I murdered her and pleaded insanity I would get away with it. Woman two (shall we call her Jenny?) would never say anything except the occasional "Yes" or "No" when Iris came up for air, which (trust me, folks) was rare. Usually by the time the story ended Jenny had run out of *yes*es and *no*s and would only acknowledge the story's end by giving a slight lopsided smile. The thing was, on every journey Iris would have a story to tell, and it mattered not whether it was all about the lovely day she had had on her day off on Sunday, or what the doctor had said about her husband's double hernia; the whole story was always punctuated with a kind of hyena-type laugh. Her laugh ran all the way through it. She could actually tell the story and laugh at the same time. No matter how funny or unfunny the story was she would tell it the same way. Then she would end the story with a kind of rattling noise – a sound a bit like putting a pound of gravel in an oil drum and pushing it down a hill. She would give a burst of four (huh-huh, huh-huh) or sometimes a burst of five (huh-huh, huh-huh, huh). Jenny would give the lopsided smile and off we would go again, this time on the subject of why her granddaughter's Halloween costume didn't fit her properly and how she had come back with fifteen packets of parma violets after an evening's trick-or-treating – huh-huh, huh-huh.

Iris-and-Jenny-type conversations, to be fair, take place on public transport between many of a certain age. I'll set the scene first for you, dear readers. Two passengers, usually retired, they can be both women or both men or even one of each. They generally sit together in the second row, sometimes the third, but never the first or the fourth.

Let's say a woman in her late forties gets on with two bags of shopping. The conversation will almost every time, with a few subtle changes, go like this:

FIRST LADY: Oh, look! D'ya see her?
SECOND LADY: No. Who are you looking at?
FIRST LADY: Her over there.
SECOND LADY: Oh, yes, I see her.
FIRST LADY: Do you know who she is? She's, er, erm, oh, wotsisname's sister, er, you know.
SECOND LADY: Is she? Never!
FIRST LADY: She is!

SECOND LADY:	Are you sure?
FIRST LADY:	Yes, and d'ya know where she's working now?
SECOND LADY:	No – go on.
FIRST LADY:	She's working in that shop – you know, the one up by the bookie's just down from the Chinese restaurant. Personally, if it was me, I wouldn't be seen dead in there let alone working in the place. But there you go, I suppose. Each to their own.
SECOND LADY:	Yes, I think I know the shop you mean, but I can't think of the name of it either.
FIRST LADY:	Course, she's married to that bloke that used to work for Curry's.
SECOND LADY:	I didn't know that. Are you sure it's him?
FIRST LADY:	Yes, absolutely.

So let's have a look. What exactly have we got, then? We have a woman, but we have absolutely no idea what her name is or who her brother is or indeed whom she is married to. We do know that her husband worked for Curry's, but what he did for them is anyone's guess. We know that she works in a shop and roughly where the shop is, although we have no idea which street it is in or even which town with any certainty. One thing we do know for sure is that the first lady wouldn't be seen dead in the joint. Despite all of this, the second lady understands exactly everything the first lady is saying to her. For the life of me, how is this possible? You know the old 'Careless talk costs lives' slogan during the war? Well, these two are living exponents of the art!

Another type of passenger is the fiddler. Fiddlers are people that don't have the slightest chance of sitting still no matter how much you bet them to do so. They will always find something to sit and fiddle with. Fiddlers can be of either sex and any age. If you have found yourself a window seat and are just sitting down for a relaxing journey home to end the day and you get a fiddler next to you, you are in big trouble. One of the worst was this woman that sat down next to me. I would say she was in her mid-twenties and she had with her a wicker bag with long handles. You know, the sort you see hanging from the side of those 'everything for the beach' sheds at the seaside. I'd noticed as she had got on that she had a distinctly worried and faraway look on her face, like something was seriously distracting her. I reckon it could have been what I am about to reveal to you, dear readers. As soon as she had sat down, the wicker bag was up on her lap. It was quite tall on her lap, so this hampered the exploration that took place. She had everything in this bag. I've been away for a long weekend to Edinburgh with less stuff than she had in this bag. The ferreting around started slowly and grew ever more frantic, almost to the point of hysteria. Every so often she would have to alter the bag's position on her lap as the frenetic rummaging gradually moved the bag across her lap and partially on to mine. A few resulting splinters of wicker were sticking into my thighs whilst others flew through the air. For well over two minutes she carried on in this way as though her life depended on it. Finally, she gave a flourish so wildly dramatic that her right elbow dug deeply into my ribcage on my left side, causing me to wince. At last she had found what she was looking for. It was small – so small that she could conceal it in her hand.

I was so tempted to say, "Please let me see it. Please let me see the wondrous thing that you have!"

She calmed down instantly, and it was almost as if the last two or three minutes hadn't happened. She then very slowly and deliberately placed the wicker bag between her knees on the floor and sat back in her seat. My imagination was now working overtime. What could it be that she had found after so much blind panic? I thought it might be a diamond ring or something made of a precious metal at the very least.

Her hand opened and there is was. It was – a strawberry-flavoured Starburst!

I do so hope that that was as big an anticlimax for you as it was for me. I couldn't believe it. After all that!

And then do you know what she did, readers? She only had the temerity to unwrap it and eat it. No apology for my bruised ribs or for my wicker-covered suit and pin-cushioned thighs or for the fact that I was now wide awake with all chance of a nap long gone! Oh, no. She just sat there with an "I've just eaten a strawberry-flavoured Starburst" contented look on her face. And then, sitting back, she enjoyed the rest of her journey. Can you imagine what I said under my breath when she got off? You can? Good! Best for me to not repeat it, then!

Another famous 'fiddling' moment was the time a large lady got on. A brief 'Oh, please don't let her sit next to me' went through my head – and she thankfully didn't. Instead she sat immediately in front of me and took out of her bag, of all things, a sewing kit. It looked to be quite a good one – the sort any lifelong fiddler would relish being able to fiddle with on the bus home. Why she took it out of her bag and decided to fiddle about with it on the bus rather than taking it home is anyone's guess. The kit was open inside a blister-sealed pack, so you could see all the accoutrements that go to make up a travelling-type sewing kit. Suddenly, she wrenched the blister seal away from the card it was glued to with such force that the sewing kit went flying through the air and landed in the aisle. Now my pointing out to you that she was a large lady is relevant because there was no way she was going to be able to lean across the seat and retrieve it from where it had landed. An elderly gent on the outside seat on the other side of the aisle decided to help out and, with a slight cry of pain as he bent down, forgetting that he couldn't bend down that far, he managed to get his hand on it. He pulled his hand back sharply as he stabbed his finger on a pair of scissors that had worked loose during the kit's flight. He managed to pick the kit up at the second attempt. By now a line of passengers six-strong was blocking the aisle. They had all stopped between getting on the bus and finding themselves a seat whilst this little 'sketch' was taking place. The elderly gent handed the kit back without a single word passing between them, and the lady held it open in front of her. She jiggled the scissors back into place and stared long and hard at all the nice things she had got in her sewing kit.

At last the time came to close it up. This was done by zipping the case up on three sides. Easy, readers? Oh, no, it wasn't! For the next ten minutes she did everything to work out how it was possible for the case to close. From where I was I could see that the zip wasn't broken, although she had jiggled and tugged at it at least half a dozen times. She retrieved the blister-sealed pack and the card and read every word on it – twice. It didn't seem as if she would ever manage to close the zip.

I suddenly felt a pang. Yes, folks, I know what you are thinking, but truly I did. I leant forward and opened my mouth to speak when she suddenly stopped and made a half-turn towards a double seat further back on the other side of the bus, two rows back from where the elderly gent was sitting. On this seat sat a young couple munching what looked like a Big Mac and chips each. She lifted her head and sniffed the air like a Bisto kid, then she threw the sewing kit along with its discarded blister seal and card into her bag, shuffled out of her seat and went upstairs. The whole thing from stopping fiddling with her purchase to vanishing up the semi-spiral staircase took about ten seconds. I still had my mouth open.

I closed it along with my eyes and muttered, "Unbelievable!"

The last 'fiddler' incident that I have to recount concerns a young woman with a bus timetable. She had this timetable in every conceivable position and folded in every possible way as we trundled our way home one early summer evening. She turned it first this way and then that. She even managed to scrape my left cheek with it on one occasion as the bus lurched forward. Finally, she found the bus she was looking for and folded the timetable to suit. She then traced with her finger the bus times whilst also moving her other hand to match it against the stops the bus made. As a final check she looked out of the window to confirm that the stops outside matched the place names on her timetable. For fifteen minutes she did this three-way check before, in a low and very calm voice, she asked me, "Is this the bus to Folkestone?"

Now, readers, how would you explain to her that she was on a bus heading forty miles in a totally different direction? Well, I bottled it as well.

"Erm, no. This is going to Margate," I spluttered.

"Oh! Oh!" she said and, in a mad flourish, rang the bell and got off at the next stop.

I'm guessing that she caught a bus back, but I will probably never know. I felt a bit sorry for her, but she could have checked the destination on the front of the bus. And what did she ask the driver for when he issued her a ticket?

You cannot fault the entertainment value of it all. You would think that people would just get on to a bus, sit themselves down and get up when they reach their stop or when the bus reaches the end of its journey. I've got to say in most cases this is true, but as you can see from what I've written there are a few passengers who seem totally unable to manage it!

I will finish this section by describing one of the funniest incidents I have ever experienced. I was sitting on the bus next to the window with a lady (a regular traveller) sitting in the seat in front of me doing her regular crossword. She was clearly not a sleeper like I was! An elderly couple were in the last half a dozen people to get on to the bus. The woman sat next to the lady in front of me and the gent made himself comfortable on one of the three tip-up seats on the other side of the aisle, resting a shopping bag on the middle seat whilst a young man occupied the third seat. OK, then, the scene is set. Off we went and everything was fine. There was nothing to suggest what was about to happen. After ten minutes or so we arrived at the bus stop adjacent to a very large supermarket and two very old ladies got on to the bus along with several bags of shopping from the aforesaid supermarket. The best part of two minutes was then taken up with them looking for their bus passes. With the passes eventually found and the tickets issued, they proceeded to make their way down the bus. The first lady stopped and, turning to the second lady, stated quite firmly, "I will sit here." She barged her way down the bus before taking up an aisle seat.

Lady number two now embarked on one of the most disruptive seating rearrangements I have ever witnessed. The elderly gent, with a swaying motion caused by the swaying of the bus (which

23

had now shut its doors and moved off, I hasten to add), got to his feet, clutching two bags of shopping in his right hand and gathering the third from the seat between himself and the young man. Ms Disruptive, wearing a most dreadful patterned headscarf, looked on not quite understanding what the elderly gent was intimating, but to the rest of us he was obviously doing the chivalrous and gentlemanly thing and letting her have his seat. She stood there looking on and a dawn of realisation spread over her face. She was then suddenly thrown into total confusion when the young man sprang to his feet and offered her his seat too! So with this embarrassment of riches of three seats to choose from, you'd think it would have been easy. But no way! She made a movement towards the seats, but she didn't know which one to choose and an impromptu do-si-do now took place between the three of them at the bottom of the stairs. They all literally encircled each other three times. The only thing missing was that they didn't link arms and shout, "Yee-har!" Then it was suddenly as if the music stopped. On the next turn round the young man sat back down on his seat again, leaving our senior citizens to share the last dance together. They circled once more round, still clutching their shopping, and then the old lady with the now slightly lopsided headscarf sat herself down on the far end of the tip-up seats and rested her shopping on the middle seat in much the same way as the elderly gent had. Why they couldn't both have sat down, holding their bags of shopping in front of them, I have absolutely no idea!

I gave a surreptitious look around the bus to see if anyone else had seen what I had just seen, but it didn't look like anyone had. So, for verification purposes, I leant forward and, in a low whisper, said to the woman in front of me, "You couldn't make it up, could you?"

Without turning round, she shook her head and said firmly, "No, you couldn't."

Do you think it ends there? Of course it doesn't. We hadn't gone another 100 yards before Ms Disruptive, with headscarf now readjusted, reached across and dinged the bell for the bus to stop. The first lady got up from her aisle seat and made her way down the bus, collecting Ms Disruptive on the way, and they got off the bus a little under a mile after they had got on. Apart from the last 100 yards, it was one of the most hilariously entertaining of the troops performances I had ever witnessed.

I have mentioned only a small selection of the things that can happen on your average bus journey, but this book would be like *War and Peace* if I were to recount them all.

In the same vein, I'm quite partial to the occasional day trip on a coach, and I have visited several places (and, indeed, countries) with a local coach firm. Coaches bring together a very different bunch of people from your average bus load. Most coach journeys are uneventful and go as planned with only a slight change to the printed schedule, and everyone on board takes it without so much as a grumble. So I can honestly say that there isn't as much to see as there is on the daily double-decker.

Anyway, for those of you that don't know, the coach usually calls at various pick-up points in several towns before heading off to its destination, and one trip stands out in my memory for three reasons. The first is that when we arrived at a pick-up point the couple we were due to pick up weren't there. We were a few minutes early so it wasn't too surprising, but we soon became ten minutes late. Suddenly the husband appeared round the corner, pointed at the coach and looked back down the road he had just come out of. He was obviously telling his wife that the coach was still there. He walked briskly towards us and got on without a word of apology or explanation. He showed the driver their tickets and took his seat. His wife, meanwhile, had followed him in that 'walk a few steps, run a few steps and then walk a few steps' manner that women often have when they're trying to hurry.

She climbed the steps of the coach as if they were the north face of the Eiger, and in a breathless voice managed to say, "I'm sorry."

Clearly feeling that this wasn't enough of an explanation for her tardiness, with a gulp of air she gave a more complete explanation: "I am sorry we're late. It was all my fault. I was brushing my teeth, you see, and I got some toothpaste in my eye." Now, I'm not saying that this is difficult, but, speaking from my own experience, over the best part of half a century I've never got toothpaste in my eye!

So with us all safely on board we were off on our day trip to Cambridgeshire.

Suddenly, without warning, the woman in front of me turned round and totally and utterly unprompted said, "I'm going to Ostend next week." I didn't have a chance to answer before she turned back and faced the front, never to speak to me again or to anyone else for the rest of the journey both there and back. Very strange! Put that one in the definitely weird category, methinks.

On the same trip there was a bloke who never shut up. You know the sort. It doesn't matter how much the rest of the coach ignores him, it doesn't matter how little a response he gets from the person who has now become his new best friend across the aisle, he never, but never, shuts up. Well, this bloke on this trip was all that and more. It was absolutely astounding. Where he had been and what he had done when he'd got there was incredible enough; who or what he had seen left nothing new for the rest of us mortals to look at. And there was no one left in the world for him to tell just where they'd been going wrong all these years, because he'd already spoken to them. You cannot imagine, readers, just how much we all basically owe our lives to this man, and this man alone. Even the coach driver at a 'comfort stop' felt the need to say something to me as we got off the coach.

"Bet you're having a fun journey where you're sitting," he said.

I suggested that he tell us all fifteen minutes and this bloke twenty minutes so that we could sneak away, leaving him behind. The driver hinted that he was seriously tempted, but then muttered something about contractual obligations, etc., etc.

Really, you cannot believe just how much complete and utter tripe issued forth from this man's cakehole. If there was ever a case for justifiable homicide, then this was it!

Chapter 3

Transports of Delight, Part 2:
The Runaway Train Went over the Hill

My first experience of train travel was when I was aged three and a half months old in my pram in the guard's van. Now, I say experience, but to be honest I've no memory of this (which I suppose I wouldn't have really), so you will just have to accept the fact, as I have, that that's when it was. Something must have clicked, as trains have always had a peculiar fascination with me. I've never wanted to be an engine driver; and no, I'm not, nor have ever been, a trainspotter! They've just always been there for a day out, and the best days out were always the ones where a train was added. Holidays, of course, and even the odd night out, have that extra touch of glamour about them when combined with a trip on Britain's premier form of land travel.

As a child, I can remember my father commuting 'up the line' to work, and I always thought that perhaps one day I would do the same. When I was aged sixteen that became the case, although the trip I used to have to take was not a very long one. However, at nineteen my job destination changed, and this meant a longer trip. An hour and a half each way, Monday to Friday, was the norm.

OK, then, first things first: I have a question. All the commuters among you will know what I am talking about, so you might be able to help; but if you aren't a commuter, I'm guessing that your response will be purely conjecture. Ready? Here goes: how is it that everyone has their own designated standing place on the platform? 'Tis true. Once you have established that a particular spot is yours, then it remains yours for all eternity. I always like it best when you turn up on a Monday morning to find that the 'stander' six feet from you is missing and that is the way it continues right through the week. Just when you think you will never see him again, he suddenly reappears looking all healthy and tanned and you just can't help thinking to yourself, 'I wonder where he's been to on his holidays, then.'

The train I used to catch in the morning was usually pretty much empty when I got on but would fill up gradually as we pursued our journey along the line. It was generally filled with two types of people: sleepers and newspaper readers. As you can guess, readers, I was a sleeper and that carried through to my 'bussing' days, which you have already read about. Apart from the fact that they were all commuting, the other major thing that they all had in common was that nobody spoke. On almost every journey I commuted on, it was as if someone had pressed the mute button on the handset, and apart from the occasional turn of the page of the *Financial Times* or *Telegraph* the silence was, as they say, deafening. If someone did speak, the look of total disdain that person then received from the seasoned commuter would have been enough to stop a town-hall clock.

The train home had exactly the same collection of people – sleepers, newspaper readers and nobody speaking. The twist for me was that I usually had to stand. The train had come from London Victoria and so was packed and heaving to bursting point before it had even left the station, let alone by the time it reached me twenty minutes into its journey. Of course I'm referring to the days of 'slammers'. As the door opened there was a collective outpouring of breath from the people crammed inside, giving the impression that they were in a mobile Black Hole of Calcutta. Somehow (and please don't ask me how, because it ranged some days from the polite to the downright rude) I would manage to squeeze on. Let's just say I used a combination of black looks, elbows and knees. I would find myself a square foot of carriage to stand on, and there I would remain for the next hour or so. The black looks expressed inward pleading – "Please, I just want to get home" – but they weren't usually enough on their own to get me to my salubrious standing position squeezed between the litter bin and the fire extinguisher; more forceful tactics sometimes needed to be employed.

One of the funniest incidents I can recall happened when I was chugging home one evening, shoehorned into the vestibule as usual. One chap in his fifties was somehow managing to read his *Telegraph* and, come to that, four other people were reading the *Telegraph* too – his, I mean, not their own. Two young ladies were standing talking about the weekend they had had and the one coming up they were going to have. They were both dressed immaculately in skirted suits (one a pale grey, the other a navy blue) and they gave me the impression that they both worked as PAs somewhere in the city. They were talking normally (not loud and not whispering), and along with the noise of the train engine and the rattling of the rocking carriage you would have had to concentrate hard if you wanted to listen to what they were saying. Suddenly, hardly raising her voice or pausing the conversation with her friend, 'Pale Grey' raised her left hand in the air in a 'Please, Miss, I want to be excused' manner, and said in a firm voice, "Is this anybody's?" In her hand she held the right wrist of a gent aged about fifty who had been standing to the side of her and, I'm presuming, had had his hand somewhere he shouldn't have.

No one answered her. Her friend laughed; the rest of us smirked. I can honestly say I never saw the face of anyone so red with embarrassment until that moment.

Another 'old bloke and young girl' incident I remember happened one very cold November evening. I was standing, as usual. The carriage was warm and almost everybody with a seat was asleep. Several were snoring at various decibels, some with a low mooing noise, others with a Gloucester Old Spot noise. Some were at the pneumatic-drill stage. Almost everyone else was just plain unconscious.

Two people at the opposite ends of their working lives were sitting together. She was maybe nineteen or twenty and dressed in her city suit (it was probably pale grey again; we all wore grey suits in the eighties, didn't we?). He was aged about sixty-ish, wearing brown trousers with a check sports jacket and dark waistcoat. He had started reading his newspaper when the train left Victoria, but he had passed out at some point, and most of the newspaper now lay in a crumpled mess on his lap and the rest had fallen on to the floor at his feet. This, unfortunately, made it impossible for me to read over his shoulder and to know exactly what Margaret Thatcher had told one of her ministers. She too had been reading – a Jilly Cooper, I seem to remember (no, the girl not Margaret Thatcher – try to keep up), and had also slipped into a temporary coma. The book was closed on her lap with her right thumb marking the page. They were both asleep, but not just asleep in their seats; they were snuggled up with their heads resting on each other's shoulders. Every so often, as the train jolted or swayed, one of them would stir slightly, but would then promptly nuzzle back into the neck of the other. They were like this all the way to the next station, which was quite a long run, and the jamming on of the brakes caused the young woman to wake up and sit upright, to be followed moments later by the man. Not a word was spoken between them. She looked to see where she was in her book, folded down the top corner of the page and placed the book in her handbag. His heap of a newspaper was somehow righted and folded – well, no, not really folded. Have you ever seen the mess some people get into with Ordnance Survey maps? Well, it was worse than that, but he somehow managed to cram the whole thing into his briefcase. Within two stops they had both got off, neither of them knowing just how intimate their journey home had been on the 17.04 from London Victoria. Let's put it this way, in some countries and cultures he would have had to marry her.

Me? I was just grateful to get a seat at last.

There is very occasionally someone who speaks up for the masses. Now this has happened at odd times, but the greatest of all has to be the journey home from work one very hot summer evening. I have always maintained that I don't know what is worse when commuting, the cold of the winter or the heat of the summer. At least in summer the trains are warm. However, they can become mobile saunas and this particular day was no exception. The carriage was divided in two, and the half I was in had a six-seater bench along its back wall. Facing the bench were two seats to the right and three seats to the left, leaving an off-centre aisle down the middle. I had managed to position myself next to the door on the double seat in the hope of getting any cool air that was going. Next to me sat a young lady in her city-suit finery and directly opposite her, sitting in the 'second from the right' position on the bench was her similarly dressed 'works in the city' colleague. To my knowledge there was no one standing, although every seat was taken and everyone looked very hot. Amongst our group of eleven only one was reading a newspaper. The rest of the carriage was in total silence. Everybody was wearing the 'please just get me home' look – all except these two city ladies. In fact, more precisely just the one, because the young lady opposite was only interjecting occasionally to complete a sentence, or to correct or confirm what her friend was saying. Her friend (next to me) was relentless! It went something like this:

"Yeah, so we first of all went to The Star and had a couple in there and I had a Boddingtons – never had a Boddingtons before but I have now and quite liked it – and then we went to have quick look in Debenhams but they didn't have what I was looking for so we thought about going somewhere else but couldn't think who else would have one so we decided to go to the pictures I wasn't that keen on going cos I had already seen it but it is a good film and I didn't let on that I had seen it so we went to the pictures cos he hadn't seen it and I didn't mind seeing it again and then he suggested we had something to eat so we went to McDonald's I'm not a fan of McDonald's meself I would rather go to Burger King but it was his birthday so we went to

31

McDonald's and then he suggested that we go for a drink so we went back to The Star and I was going to have a Boddingtons again but decided not to have a Boddingtons so I had something else and was going to have a Bloody Mary but I don't know what that is so had a rum and coke instead and then after we left the pub we went back to his place and cos we knew his parents were out it being Saturday and they go dog racing we knew we'd have the place to ourselves and then we, tee-hee, yeah we did and then we went downstairs to see what was on the TV but there was only some old film that we had both seen so not long afterwards I went home and then on Sunday we decided to go for a drive in the country I like being in the country and he knows I like the country so he said let's go for a drive so off we went and he suggested a country pub for lunch and I thought that was a good idea so . . ."

At that point, a lady second from the left on the bench could stand it no longer. She finally cracked under the strain and, in a very loud voice, exclaimed, "Cor, don't she ever shut up!"

No one answered her. No one needed to.

The disbelief on the girl's face that somebody had said that along with the annoyance of having her flow interrupted had to be seen to be believed.

Suddenly, she gathered her wits and forcefully replied to the woman and to the world in general: "How rude! I think that's rude. How rude is that! I can't believe that. I can't believe that someone could be that rude."

The lady with the loud voice now stated her case: "We don't want to hear it, love. We all just want to get home, and we don't want to hear all about you and your weekend or your love life."

The young lady retorted with "I wasn't talking that loudly. At least, I didn't think I was talking that loudly. Was I talking that loudly?" she said to her friend opposite, glancing at the passengers on either side of her friend, including yours truly.

The friend shrugged her shoulders and everyone else looked back at her blankly in an insolent kind of way, dumbly agreeing with the loud-voiced lady.

"Huh! How rude! Can't believe that," she muttered finally.

She then looked down at her lap – a position she stayed in for the next three stops before finally getting off. I never saw her or the spokeswoman on behalf of beleaguered commuters ever again.

Of course not all train travel for me has been as a commuter. Days out, weekends away and holidays bring a whole new experience to the train traveller – or so you might think. In Chapter 1 I told the story of one man and his dog catching the train at Reading, and these next two train tales also concern first-class rail travel between Paddington and the West Country. First-class trains from the West Country on a Monday morning usually tend to contain MPs of various parties from Cornish constituencies. They are on their way to another hard week in the House of Commons so the peace and quiet is occasionally broken by jovial banter(!). This was considered when booking a weekend in Devon, and so the decision was taken to come home on the Sunday instead.

The day was sunny and warm and the sky a deep azure. (Sorry, readers – I went all poetic there for a second.) The train rolled in on time. I hadn't booked a seat, so I muscled my way past the reserved seats and found a single seat. On the opposite side of the aisle there were four seats in two pairs with a table in between. On one of the four seats sat a gent whom at this stage I hadn't paid any attention to – yes, yes, unusual I know. The train pulled out and we were on our way. I gazed out of the window, watching the station disappearing into the distance. Suddenly, this gent cleared his throat – and I don't just mean *clear*. This was a rasping, deep-down, bowels-of-the-earth type of clearance, and it rattled the carriage windows. The sound caused me to pull a face, but I didn't change the direction in which I was facing – that is, not until he did it again if anything a tad louder than before.

My cat was dead – curiosity had killed it! I turned round and there sitting at, and I hasten to add *occupying*, all four seats and the table was a famous actor.

Now, I'm sorry, readers, but I'm not going to tell you who it was, but suffice it to say he was in a multi-Oscar-nominated film of the eighties. Yes, I know that doesn't narrow it down a great deal, but that's all you're getting.

For the next two and a bit hours this actor coughed, and generally cleared his tubes, every few minutes. It reached the point where I was imagining the next day's newspaper headline: 'Actor Murdered Because of Persistent Cough'. "I've got a frog" were his last words, the whole article being accompanied by a picture of me being led in handcuffs, upon arrival at Paddington, to Belmarsh Prison. I had visions of experts on the early evening news discussing why I'd done it: perhaps I'd been stalking him for years, just waiting for the opportunity to strangle him in carriage G of an Inter-City 125! I got the impression that he was coughing so that someone would speak to him or get him to autograph something, but no one did and the hawking nightmare continued all the way to Platform 5 at London Paddington.

The second tale of first-class woe is not nearly as bad. It starts from when I boarded the train for London at Liskeard in Cornwall. The train was fairly full and I was lucky to get a seat. I sat in a block of four seats with no one next to me and a late-middle-aged couple sitting opposite me on the other side of the table. Well, readers, we hadn't gone two miles when the gent directly opposite me moved his feet and I got a kick to the right shin. I winced slightly and moved my legs. No apology was forthcoming. He moved them again and I received another swift blow, this time to the left ankle. When I received another blow a few minutes later my glower across the table surely ought to have prompted a 'sorry'. Nope – no way! I was kicked mercilessly for the rest of Cornwall and over the Royal Albert Bridge at Saltash, until, thankfully, a fellow passenger vacated his seat at Plymouth and I was able to move my bruised lower legs to the other side of the aisle. I looked back briefly and I could see that he had now stretched his legs across the whole floor space of where I'd been sitting. Sorry, readers – I am not able to convey to you at this point exactly what words were in my head for fear of contravening this country's decency laws.

My new seating position gave me a whole new angle as it

allowed me to view down the whole length of the carriage, but, to be honest, I didn't have to look far to see something noteworthy – only as far as the next block of four seats diagonally across from where I was sitting.

She wouldn't have attracted my attention at all had she not declared in a highly affected and loud voice, "Oh, no, nothing off the trolley for me. I shall be eating Pullman class, fine dining!"

I don't know why it is, but some of the scruffiest train passengers I have ever seen are to be found in first class. Everywhere similar has a dress code (usually 'smart casual') but not, it seems, the railway network. This lady was no exception. She was wearing an old pair of trainers (and I mean *old*), scruffy jeans (and no, we're not talking 'designer' here) and a filthy shirt. She was basically dressed, I thought, courtesy of The Dogs Trust, and the whole ensemble was capped off with a hairstyle that looked like I had cut it, drunk and with my eyes shut. And yet here she was travelling first class on a train and getting up to have her luncheon – Pullman class, fine dining, don't you know! It was at this point that I decided to nod off. However, the same woman woke me up upon her arrival back at her seat.

"Would you like to move over to the window seat so that I can sit there?" she stated in an authoritative voice.

I was awake now, and I caught the indignant look on the face of the lady to whom this statement had been addressed.

"No, not really. I don't want to," came her defensive reply.

Mrs Everything Scruffy calmly announced that she had drunk at least a litre of water with her luncheon and was very likely to be 'getting up and down'.

Needless to say, the second lady moved. However, this now put her in a worse position as she was now unable to avoid getting Mrs Everything Scruffy's life story.

"My son is a management consultant in the States, don't you know. He's doing awfully well," she added. When the train slowed during the last mile into Paddington Station, she stood up, adjusted the filthy shirt and looked up at the luggage rack, where she had put her case. Then she proceeded to stand on the seat (both feet, mind) and took the case down, and no one said a thing! If she'd been sixteen and wearing a hoodie there would have been an outcry.

You see, readers, I told you it wasn't as bad as the first story, although I suppose it depends on your point of view!

Strange things don't happen only on long journeys; the short ones have their moments too. A short train journey I was once on was only going to take fifteen minutes – I mean, readers, what could go wrong? Just about everything, that's what.

The train was quite full and I found myself a seat towards the back of the carriage. I had to sit there as my first choice of seat was taken up by the coats of a couple. I would say they were in their seventies. They themselves were sitting on the other side of the aisle at a table, and the two seats opposite them were taken up with their luggage, still bearing luggage labels fastened to the handles. Another piece of luggage was blocking the aisle and a fourth piece was in the mid-carriage vestibule. I'm guessing these two liked to spread themselves out, wouldn't you agree?

The oddest thing was how they were dressed. It was as if they had both been to the Royal Command Performance, or to a regimental dinner at the very least. They were immaculately, if not a bit quaintly, dressed. Now, I'm no fashion expert, but he wasn't wearing any item of clothing that matched anything else he was wearing. His most notable garment was a yellow check waistcoat, complete with pocket watch. She was in a flimsy dress that was more Matalan than Milan. Surely they couldn't have travelled dressed like that for five hours on a plane from far-off foreign climes!

She also had what can only be described as an absolutely stinking cold, and we all had to know about it. She constantly sniffed, each sniff louder than the previous one. I was nearing the point of shouting, "For God's sake, woman, blow it!" When she started searching her handbag I thought perhaps she was looking for a clean hanky – maybe she was at first; but if she was, this was then superseded by what she did find.

"Must sort this out," she said as she held in her hand a wad of £20 notes. It was a stash of at least £400 and she was waving it around akin to how a spectator waves a flag during a royal visit. After putting it back in her handbag, she took out a note and gave it to her husband, saying to him as if he was five years old, "There's the money for the taxi." I thought she was going to add, 'and I want change,' but she didn't.

The husband looked at the note quizzically and finally declared, "Do you think the taxi driver will take this?"

A look of annoyance spread across her face. "Yes, of course he will!" she snapped. She then stared at it for several seconds until the penny dropped.

"Oh, no, he won't, will he?"

It was a 10-euro note and not a £10 note. She stuffed it back into her handbag, her hand emerging with a good old British tenner.

So then, readers, can you guess at which stop they alighted? Yes, that's the one!

As she stood up she muttered that she had indigestion, and, as that didn't get a response, she then announced to the world in general, "Ooh, I do feel queer."

I couldn't quite understand why they had three coats, considering that there were only two of them, but they along with the four cases managed to get in the way of everybody else, including the guard, as they got off the train. How at least two passengers didn't go headlong over them and the cases when the train's sliding doors opened I will never know! With a bit of slinking body movement I managed to get round the whole works and get off.

I had already booked my taxi, so I knew that it would be waiting outside the station for me; and lo and behold! there it was. The driver got out when he saw me, opened the boot, took my bags from me and placed them in it. I confirmed with him where we were going and he looked puzzled.

"That's not where I'm supposed to be going," he said in a manner that suggested I wanted him to take me to Aberdeen, wait for me and bring me back. "I'm supposed to be going to—"

Before he could finish, guess who arrived? Yes, you're right again, readers – you're getting good at this. Mrs Asian Flu was standing so close that she could have got in my coat with me. "I [sniff] think [sniff] this taxi is ours [double sniff]."

It just had to be, hadn't it?

At that precise moment a second taxi drew into the car park. The driver got out and called a cheery "Taxi for Jenkins!"

I extracted my bags from the boot of taxi number one and loaded them into the boot of taxi number two. As we drove off, I noted Mrs Asian Flu was giving the taxi driver a talking-to and rummaging in her handbag again. Perhaps she was going to show him her wad!

It had definitely been another 'glad to get in the front door' kind of day!

The people that travel on buses or trains are a breed apart. They say of some people that when they get into a car and drive it, no matter how mild-mannered they usually are, some completely different personality takes over. Well, readers, let me tell you your public-transport traveller is no different. Don't let anyone fool you otherwise. There is no way they behave in the same way in any other sphere of their life. I just won't believe it!

For me, bus and train travel have always been necessary to get me around for both work and play. I have often heard people complaining of them being late or overcrowded, and this is usually true; but there is no doubt that if you want cheap entertainment, leave the car at home and catch the bus or train. It doesn't always work – granted – but, believe me, when it does it leaves an indelible mark in your brain that only shock therapy will remove. Many of your journeys will leave you with 'look back and smile' images that will live with you for years. You will find yourself telling the stories, and they will all start with "I remember when I caught the bus once. . . ." Or you will find yourself arriving somewhere with "You are not going to believe what's just happened to me on the train. . . ."

So come on – join me. Go and find yourself a bus stop; shuffle forward and when the bus arrives get your toes trodden on in the process; get on; get yourself a ticket and a good seat, and sit back and enjoy the ride of your life. It's cheaper than the pictures;

you have got the best seat in the house and this movie is never ever predictable. Oh, and don't forget to buy yourself a return ticket, because, you never know, the journey back could be even better.

So come on – join me. Go and find yourself a train station; ask at the booking office for a timetable (a quid says they ain't got one); find a train to somewhere (anywhere); check to see how late it's running; find yourself a spot on the platform (preferably not a commuter's designated standing place) and relax. Squeeze yourself on (or you never know your luck, you might even get a seat) and let your journey unfold. Don't do a me and nod off. Concentrate and enjoy the lunacy going on around you. And don't forget your return ticket, for the same reason as above.

Good luck, readers, and happy hunting. There's a world out there, and public transport is ready and waiting to take you to it. Here's to the hope that you too have the kind of journeys that make you appreciate just how good it is to get in your front door and close it behind you!

Chapter 4

Plane Sailing

Many people are terrified of flying. Some are terrified of the take-off, some of the landing, some of both. If you are one of these people, you have my sympathy. I, however, find the whole experience of flying enjoyable and exhilarating. However, it does bring together an extremely weird and altogether strange bunch of people.

The only way I can describe this to you is to take you, dear readers, through it all step by step. I wouldn't say that I'm your most frequent flyer, but I can admit to travelling round the world to far-flung destinations, and I can honestly say that when it comes to checking-in there has never really been an occasion that stands out. There is, of course, always someone who, after queuing for maybe the best part of an hour, is not holding their ticket in their hand when they reach the desk. How is this possible? They must know where they are and what they're about to do. You have probably all seen TV programmes with people 'losing it' at the check-in. Well, I guess I've always been lucky at this stage of the journey, although I am sure there are hundreds of you out there with check-in nightmares to tell!

Anyway, no matter – you're through and on your way. Next stop: the shopping mall. This always seems to be a relatively quiet place with just a general hubbub. It is never particularly loud. What I mean is it's hardly Lakeside on a Saturday afternoon, is it? And again I cannot put my finger on one single 'Why on Earth?' or 'I wonder what's gone on here' moment whilst browsing round Waterstones or Tie-Rack.

With check-in and a mosey round the shops done, the next usual thing is to grab something to eat.

Oh dear! Sitting in the eating area at an airport are some of the most downcast, depressed and miserable people I have ever laid my eyes on. Granted, they may have been up very early, they may have had a long drive and they may have had a three-hour check-in, but come on! Most of them are going on their holidays to far-off sunnier climes; they're escaping from work, the boss, the neighbours, the British weather, the in-laws, maybe even the kids; and they're off for two weeks to the sun-kissed shores of a tropical isle! I have never seen someone on their way to the gallows (and indeed, I'm never likely to), but surely they couldn't look unhappier than this! The complete misery that exudes from the faces of these people is a joy to behold. How can they be so unhappy going on a holiday they've spent eleven and a half months saving up for?

This progresses in the departure lounge, where, judging by the look on their faces, they seem to be hoping their solicitor will burst through the door at any moment with a stay of execution. But no – the call comes and they have got to go and get on their plane. Personally, I would rather be stretched out on a beach in Crete than have two weeks in Bognor Regis in November, though try telling their faces that!

So, it's done: we've checked in, done the shops, had a bacon-and-Brie ciabatta and sat in the departure lounge. We've been called, and now we're on the plane, in our seats, fiddling with our cushions and our blankets and wishing they would bring the headphones round earlier. We then have instructions about what to do should the plane crash. I don't know why it is, but I always have a smile to myself when they demonstrate 'with whistle and light'. I suppose it's the thought of having someone who's not seen or heard the plane crash but can hear you blowing your whistle whilst bobbing about in the Atlantic wearing a Mae West!

I tend to watch the film (even if I know it, chapter and verse), listen to music or, best of all, sleep my way through most of the journey except when troughing my in-flight meal or being woken up and asked if I'd like a drink by the flight attendant. Once on the way to Singapore I swear if I'd said yes every time she asked, I wouldn't have known where I was for at least two days after I'd got off.

Ah yes – the in-flight meal that has been specially prepared by some semi-famous chef or other! How is it that whenever you are served a drink on a plane it is at that precise moment that the plane flies through turbulence? I've worn the complimentary glass of wine of the person next to me on more than one occasion, I can tell you. And why is it that wherever I have sat on a plane the trolley runs out just as it gets to me and they have to wheel it all the way back to replenish it? It matters not if they are coming up the aisle towards me or from behind, I reckon I'm always in the last half a dozen to get my scoff.

Then there is always this conversation usually two or three rows in front of me:

"Would you like the pork or the chicken?" says the attendant.

"Haven't you got beef?" is the reply.

This always seems to come from a bloke aged over forty and wearing a sports jacket. It could be my imagination, of course, so I need you, readers, to keep an eye out and confirm for me that it is this gent that without fail has this inane conversation. Where was I? Oh, yes.

"Haven't you got beef?"

"No, it's just chicken or pork," says the attendant firmly.

"Are you sure? You had beef last time I flew with you," says our man.

"Maybe, but it's chicken or pork this time," says the attendant firmly again, her ever present smile slipping slightly.

"I saw that it was on the menu as chicken or pork, but I thought perhaps you'd have beef," says Mr Annoying.

"No, it's chicken or pork." The attendant is by now holding one of each with a look of 'make a choice or you'll be wearing both' on her face.

"Oh, erm, well, I suppose I'd better have the pork, then, if that's all you've got," he says finally.

"No, we do also have chicken," the attendant says, unbelievably. I mean, folks, wouldn't you just dump it on his tray and walk away?

"Oh, I didn't realise you had chicken[!]. No, no – it's OK. I'll have the pork."

He then proceeds to tell the person next to him (whether they are his travelling companion or not) all about the fact that (a) he's not fond of pork, and (b) they had beef last time he flew with them. He finally ends with "This is very nice, isn't it?"

Of course, I am sitting two rows back, my face a study in disbelief, and I already know what I am going to get.

"Sorry, sir, we've run out. I'll just pop back and get some more. Would you like another drink while you're waiting?"

Hic!

At last we reach our destination. We're starting to make our approach. The tray is up; the seat is in an upright position. The ground comes whizzing up very fast, there is a slight squeal of tyres and we're down. We taxi our way to the terminal, and then I will never understand what happens next if I live to be 115. The 'Seat Belt On' sign goes off!

Now, we've all seen the first day of Harrods' sale; there are those who sit outside the doors from Christmas Eve in the hope of getting that £300 canteen of cutlery for a tenner; and when those doors open there is a flood of people that dash in, making it look like an end-of-the-world sale and not just Harrods. Well, the same thing happens as soon as that little LED goes out. The belts come off and they're up, hand luggage retrieved from the overhead lockers, and there they are in a line down the aisle, waiting to get off, looking for all the world like that famous 'Labour Isn't Working' billboard from the late 1970s. The engine noise can still be heard at this point. Will someone please, please explain to me what they are hurrying for? The doors aren't open and I have never yet seen, anywhere in the world, baggage handlers ready and waiting to unload a plane, and yet it seems to me that everyone makes a mad dash to get off the plane.

43

Everyone wants to be first to the carousel to get their suitcase, though clearly it's not going to be there! I can honestly say that I have been in the last half a dozen people to get off a plane more times than I care to remember and I have never yet missed out on my place in the great carousel huddle.

This brings us to passport control, and, like checking in, I have never experienced a great problem with this (excepting one time when a swarthy-looking gent was led away in Majorca). I'm usually at the back of the queue, as I'm usually one of the last off the plane. This brings us to learning your ABC – that's the Airport Baggage Claim!

See the above 'Labour Isn't Working' comment, because now we have the same line of people standing next to a lifeless luggage carousel. All conversation is spoken in a low murmur, and after a few anxious looks at watches and several peeks at the carousel number to make sure they've got the right one, everyone suddenly sparks into life as the first suitcase bursts out from the hole in the middle. It is followed by hundreds more bags and suitcases of all shapes and sizes, with the odd pushchair or stroller thrown in for good measure. I can never get the voice out of my head from *The Generation Game* that says, "And on the conveyer belt tonight we have . . ."

Have you ever noticed that the people who have made the dash and have arrived there long before you have are always still there after you have collected your suitcase or bag and gone? And then the opposite: the man who arrives from nowhere, pushes his way through the crowd thronging the carousel (none of whom are standing behind the line, I hasten to add), picks up his bag and is gone, all in less than twenty seconds from start to finish! Then there's the bloke who manages to capture his huge case and wrestles it from the carousel, over the protecting lip and on to the ground, knocking out of the way (and sometimes almost over) two or three fellow passengers. With the huge case now lying dead and motionless on the floor, he reads the label only to discover it isn't his. The whole rigmarole is then conducted in reverse, and a minute later there it is back on the carousel.

Now, I am very sorry, ladies – I'm not normally sexist, but I do have to be at this point. Gents, if you have ever flown with your missus, have you ever noticed how you tend to get separated at the ABC, usually with you on one side and her on the other? This is a cleverly orchestrated ploy so that, when the bags come round on the carousel, she can lean forward and, without getting her hands dirty or (God forbid!) breaking a nail, read the label on the suitcase as it goes past her, look up at you and, in a combination of hand movements and exaggerated mouthing, say, "That's our one there." You can then guarantee that the bag in front of it belongs to the bloke standing next to you (who has probably had the same instruction mouthed to him). He then proceeds to make such a meal of getting his own suitcase off that yours passes you by. When you've gone and missed the chance of snatching it, there is a rolling of the eyes and much head-shaking from the memsahib across the divide.

Everybody who is a regular flyer must surely have a nightmare story to tell. Well, mine has to be the journey home from the lovely Caribbean island of St Kitts. I won't bore you, readers, with all the gory details, but suffice it to say that the journey home involved flying to Antigua before flying to Heathrow. However, the plane was so late leaving St Kitts that the connection was missed at Antigua and five of us were stranded overnight. The next day we had to fly to Barbados first and then to London. A tour of the Caribbean wasn't planned, but we had one anyway. As I said, I'm not going to bore you with the gory details, but when I said there were five of us stranded it was actually twelve. The five of us stood in disbelief with our mouths open as this one family, having arrived with us in Antigua, and having found the plane gone, immediately got themselves on the next flight to England. That's somewhere in England – not London Heathrow. And although their luggage had been unloaded from the St Kitts plane, they quickly decided that's where they would leave it – in the terminal at Antigua. We're not just talking a holdall here; we are talking about seven people with at least two suitcases each, several small bags, a fold-up Mclaren pushchair for their two-year-old plus innumerable sundry items. I'm guessing that they got home, but how much of their luggage ever did? I'll probably never ever know. This story clearly contradicts all my other observations of the ABC!

Of all the possible ways of getting from A to B, can there be a better way than climbing into a tin can and being whizzed off through the clouds? Far-off destinations can be reached in just a few hours – places that took our ancestors weeks full of trials and tribulations to get to. There's no way you could change my opinion of flying – there just isn't.

So, the next time, readers, after you've checked in, bags gone, and are enjoying a preflight bacon sarnie and you can't wait any longer for your two weeks in the Balearics, stop and look about you at the pictures of misery going on their holidays too. You will see what I mean. Get yourself on the plane to be greeted by the smiling stewardesses. And make the most of that moment because you won't see anyone else smiling on this trip – or any other, come to that. Make sure that you have an in-flight meal just so you can listen out for the 'chicken or pork' discussion. I'm not making this up – it really does happen! And, of course, you must be ready for when the plane touches down and the stampede which follows that little light going out. And will you promise me that you will be thinking of me as you muscle your way into the luggage-carousel huddle? Now, no butting, no gouging and no hitting below the belt! Find and grab that case before the missus spots it, bundle it off the carousel, and get yourself away as quickly as you can and off to 'Purple Parking'!

Chapter 5

A Table for Two and a Portion of Chips

There is little doubt that on occasion we all like to put the frying pan away and let someone else do the cooking for a change. You can always send out for a takeaway. How about trying out that new Chinese? You know – the one that poked their menu through your front door the other day. Or, better still, why not have a wander down to your local chippie? Friday and Saturday nights are everybody's favourite takeaway nights – aren't they? – and I am no exception.

Sending out for a Chinese or a pizza breaks the regularity of 'going down the chippie', but to me there is no question: the sheer enjoyment of standing in a chip shop with all its heavenly smells cannot be equalled by any other food-serving establishment. Almost everybody eats chips, and even those who can't eat chips would eat them if they could. Equally, the diversity of clientele of your average chip shop is not rivalled in any other place I have ever been in. Every age group, every size and shape, every hair colour and every class in our society is there, because nothing in this world brings British people together better than a bag of chips. However, it seems to me that it's not always as simple as it might be. I have seen grown-up, sensible people go to pieces in a chip shop. Is it the smell? Is it the occasion? Let me give you a few examples.

First of all – does this happen to anybody else? – I have lost count of the number of times I have been within thirty yards of a chip shop when suddenly out of nowhere someone appears and goes into the shop right in front of me. It's almost as if they have suddenly appeared out of another dimension to delay me on my quest for a jumbo sausage and chips. Now, don't get me wrong, readers – this doesn't happen every time, just *nearly* every time. And why does it always seem to be raining when, the one time that it does happen, our fourth-dimension time traveller pinches the last standing position in the shop and I'm the one left standing out on the pavement?

At last the person at the front of the queue gets served and I'm inside the shop. And they are all there. There's the city gent who has just got off the train and has popped in on his way home; there's the lads that normally hang round the shopping precinct, who have come in for a warm; there's the little girls fresh from dance class with their mum, still wearing their costumes and dancing pumps; there's the blokes fresh off the building site, still wearing their hard hats and high-visibility jackets; and then there's the odd pensioner who, like me, is keeping the Friday-night-down-the-chippie tradition alive.

So one by one they all get served. Oh, if only it were that easy! The precinct lads are first, and there's no trouble: a cone of chips each and a vigorous shaking and spraying of salt and vinegar and they leave the shop, giving us a chance to shuffle along.

The building-site blokes are next up.

"Eight cod 'n' chips please, love," says the first one.

"You're working late," replies the, as yet, unhurried and unfazed Mrs Wrapper-upper behind the counter.

"Yeah, gotta big job on round the corner, ain't we? And we're taking advantage of the nice wevva while we've got it," the senior white hard hat says in clarification of his order – an order that now gets put on hold as a cry from the chip fryer states firmly in a voice of doom that "Cod'll be five minutes!"

Our ballerinas are next, and they too have an easy order: two small cones of chips. Mum sighs as she realises she'll have to 'break a twenty' cos she didn't know they were going to be that much!

The five minutes have now elapsed, and the cods are flying into the heated cabinet at a rate of knots. To wrap up eight cod 'n' chips takes a while, not helped when confusion reigns as to which is having salt and vinegar, which is having just salt and which is having just vinegar.

A few more enter the shop, and the door is now wide open as the six-o'clock rush has started.

The senior hard hat has now got his order and stands back. Until this moment, hard hat number two hasn't spoken, but now he does with an order that can only be likened to a Richard Attenborough Oscar-acceptance speech. "Er, yeah, er, can I get er, one 'addock and chips, two plaice and chips, two, er, pies (I fink the chicken-and-mushroom ones'll do) and, er, oh, have you got any mushy peas? Oh no, I can see you ain't got that on your menu. Oh, well, er, never mind. Can I have two battered sausages (er, er, jumbo ones, I fink), six portions of chips, three portions of onion rings, four pickled eggs and a couple o'wallies? Cheers, love!"

She's not unfazed any longer. I couldn't believe it either. Why do they put clocks in fish-and-chip shops? Surely it must be only so that you can see how long you've been waiting. For those of you keeping count, I've been waiting an irritating twelve minutes already. And then comes a lifesaver: the voice of doom emerges from the depths a second time.

"Onion rings will be five minutes. They're out the back and I will have to go and fetch 'em," Mrs Wrapper-upper announces quite firmly. "I will wait until they're done before doing the rest of the order."

Surely, then, readers, this means the rest of us can get served in the next five minutes!

The city gent shuffles into position at the counter and in a plummy voice announces, "Can I have a large haydock [I thought that was the name of a racecourse] and a large portion of fries [I thought you only had those in McDonald's], if you would be so kind, please?"

No one speaks, although a few eyebrows are raised all round and Mrs Wrapper-upper dispatches his order with lightning speed. It's nearly my turn, readers. There's only the pensioner in front of me, clutching a crumpled tenner. The hard-hat boys are now standing to one side, muttering.

"You know where it says *pensioners' fish and chips* on your menu – what's the difference between a pensioner's cod and a small cod? Is it that the pensioner's small cod is smaller than a small cod or is it that it is bigger than a small cod and not as big as a big cod?" says our elderly gent, who clearly does not want to be done out of a couple of extra fork-fuls of fish.

"It's slightly smaller than a small cod, and boneless," says an agitated Mrs Wrapper-upper.

"So when you say smaller, how much smaller? If it's not much smaller, I might as well have a small cod for an extra twenty pence."

Mrs Wrapper-upper exhales a long breath and doesn't appear to breathe back in again. She walks over to the heated cabinet and emerges with tongs in each hand, each one clasping a piece of cod. "That's the difference," she says.

"Which is which?" he replies.

"That's the small one," she says with attitude, jiggling her left hand in the air.

"Oh, I see. Tell you what: I'll have a large cod and me and my wife will have half each."

Groan.

"Which ones are the cods?" he requests, poking at the heated cabinet with a long, bony index finger.

"Those three are," states Mrs Wrapper-upper, her gaze now looking over his shoulder to the ever lengthening queue down the street, which has now almost reached the aptly named Curl Up and Dye hairdresser's on the corner.

"I'll have that one, then," he says finally, "and two portions of chips, please."

The voice of doom speaks forth again: "Chips will be five minutes – got a big order on here, don't ya know."

The world now goes into suspended animation as we all wait

50

for more chips. Finally they're ready, and Mr Pensioner has his large cod and double chips.

It's me next! Or is it? The onion rings must be ready and I just know that I'm going to have to sit through pickled eggs and wallies before it's my turn.

"Onion rings are done. Two portions, right?" states the voice of doom from the chip fryer.

"No, mate. I need three – don't I? – not two," says hard hat number two.

"I'll put you some more on, then. Sorry about that," announces Mr Doom.

Mrs Wrapper-upper looks at me briefly and I seize the glance!

"Large cod and chips and a jumbo sausage and chips, please," I blurt out, somewhat unintelligibly as I haven't spoken for over twenty minutes. I am just grateful that I still have the power of speech.

Without batting an eyelid, she whizzes through my order, snatches the money out of my hand and we are done. From order to change in my outstretched palm has taken less than thirty seconds, although I have been in the shop for thirty minutes!

I hack and slice my way through the crowd in the doorway, and outside are police with riot shields and crush barriers – no, I've made that bit up. I don't bother to stop and count just how many make up the by now very bedraggled and miserable-looking throng. I put my hood up and my head down and make my way home.

I started this chapter by saying, 'Why not have a wander down to your local chippie?' Well, better still, how about trying out your local restaurant? What possible disaster could befall you there? What could be nicer than having a quiet and cosy meal for two with a loved one in a restaurant you know well, where the food is always nice and the staff are always friendly and welcoming? What indeed! But that's where it goes wrong. People don't like the comfortable-pair-of-slippers approach; they gamble with their night out by going to "you know – that new place that looks really nice from the outside and has those bushes by the door". She's seen it advertised in the local paper and she's driven past it, and that's usually enough to find yourself standing outside the place at eight o'clock on a blowy Saturday night in October. One quick look at the menu on the window, and before you know it you're standing at a 'Please Wait Here to Be Seated' sign.

Sure enough a smiling waitress arrives with a cheery "Table for two, is it?" and with two menus off the pile she heads off on a guided tour of the restaurant with us in pursuit. She goes more quickly than if the fire alarm is clanging and we all have to evacuate the building. We finally arrive at a table. Have you ever noticed how it's always the last table you would have picked, even if you'd had a choice of every table in the place.

"Just got here, have you?" A voice comes from somewhere in the dark corner to my left.

It belongs to a man aged about fifty, who is having dinner with a lady – presumably his wife. Be proud of me – I resist the sarky urge.

"Yes, first time we've been here. Looked nice so thought we'd give it a try."

"Yeah, that's what we thought, twenty minutes ago. Not seen anyone since. Ain't even had a drink yet."

A waitress appears, empty-handed, and walks through the space between me and Mr and Mrs Grump. Several minutes pass and she makes the return journey, but this time she is headed off.

"Any chance of a drink here, love?" Mr Grump sardonically requests. "Been waiting for over twenty minutes, you know."

"Certainly, sir. What would you like?" comes her sweet oh-looks-like-I've-got-a-right-one-here reply.

"Oh, don't know," he says.

I mean, it's not like he hadn't had the time to plan it, had he?

"Have you got a wine list?" he decides at last.

"I'll fetch it for you," says the waitress, and off she skips to fetch it.

Two minutes go by before I am roped in again by Mr Grump: "Probably gonna have to wait twenty minutes for that now, I suppose."

Ten minutes later there's still no wine list and his immediate circle of friends has now been extended beyond me to just about anybody in earshot.

"Come on, Alice – that's it. Can't wait any longer. Might as well go down the chippie [see – every time] and pop in the offie than hang about here any longer. Cor, what a dump! Won't be coming back here again."

With that, Mr and Mrs Grump noisily scrape their chairs and head off into the night, mumbling, never to be seen or heard of there again. I've not seen them down the chippie either.

Less than a minute later the cheery waitress arrives with the wine list.

"Don't worry," I say, "they've gone. I'll have it, though."

She is back five minutes later and we have a nice, slow, relaxing and enjoyable meal. However, that's not the end of it – well, it wouldn't be, would it? After the Grumps have gone, their seat is taken by Mr and Mrs Whinge. What these two do not find to moan about isn't worth mentioning. They moan, whine, whinge and tut through the entire meal and criticise everything that is served to them.

"Don't like the look of that."

"Reckon it's gone off."

"I'm sure they've overcooked this."

"I'm sure it shouldn't look like that."

"Blimey, where's the rest of it?"

"Didn't know you could serve this with that and with those scattered all over it."

Their big chance comes about fifteen minutes into the meal. The cheery waitress comes back with "Is everything all right for you both?" and I fear the worst. I am ready for Mr Whinge's tirade to be released. But what do you think he says, readers?

"Ooh, yes, thanks. It's really lovely." He couldn't have sounded more sincere.

She hasn't been gone a minute when suddenly I hear, "Does yours taste like vulcanised rubber too?"

Luckily, by this stage, we'd finished. I pay and leave our tip, which I notice Mr Whinge also tuts at. The last thing I hear him say to Mrs Whinge is "Don't think for one minute I'm going to be leaving 'em a fiver."

One of the best restaurant experiences that I feel everybody should experience at least once in their lives is the office/works Christmas do. If I were to put an advert in the paper asking for people's Christmas-do experiences, I would be inundated with replies. I'd probably have enough material from this subject alone to write another book as a follow-up to this one. What I always love is that, no matter whom you work for, Christmas parties always tend to follow the same pattern every year. There are the people that never come; there are the people that come, but only have orange juice, water or coke because they're driving (as it's once a year, you'd think that they could catch the bus or at least share a taxi); and there are the people who always say their dinner is worse than everybody else's. Then there's always the five-minute speech by the boss, who then within twenty minutes of delivering it exits stage left. There then follows the half-hour discussion about the drinks bill. I say 'discussion', although 'row' is probably a more appropriate word.

"I don't see why I should pay twenty quid. I only had a coke," says one.

"Well, I only had a water," says another.

"Gawd, hic, knows what I've, hic, had," says a third as he slumps down in his chair.

Many mutterings and murmurings later and, after scrabbling round for loose change, the party organiser walks gingerly over to the till, her hands cupping several hundred pounds in cash.

With the meal done and dusted for another year, there's always the last six or seven hardcore revellers who manage to drag a two-hour meal out for five or six hours. The evening can only finish with flaming sambucas, tears, vomit and hangovers and maybe even a trip to Boots for a pregnancy-testing kit. Don't ask – nothing to do with me!

The hardcore revellers tend to finish the evening somewhere else – usually somewhere one of them knows well, but most of the rest have never been to or even heard of. I'm not talking about your nice, quiet country pub with a roaring log fire that only sees the occasional walker or Old Bert popping in with his dog, Scamp, for his nightly half a Guinness, nor your average pub where all the staff and customers know one another and a convivial and ambient atmosphere is enjoyed by all. No, I'm talking about your push-and-shove pub, where it takes twice as long to get served as it does to actually drink the drink you've been standing at the bar waiting for, for twenty minutes whilst waving a tenner at the bar staff every time they walk past. This kind of pub will sometimes have an altercation too that goes something like this:

"'Ere, mate, what d'ya fink you're looking at?"

"Nuffin', mate. Wasn't lookin' at nuffin'."

"Yeah, you were. You was lookin' at my bird. I saw ya."

"No, I wasn't."

"Yeah, don't give me that. You was. I saw ya."

"You got it wrong, mate. I wasn't looking at her. I wouldn't be looking at her anyway because—"

"What are you sayin'? Are you sayin' my bird's ugly and you wouldn't want to look at her? Are ya? Are ya?"

That's the 'time to go' line. Unless you want a ringside seat to a free boxing match you need to be somewhere else within the next ten seconds.

And so another Christmas do comes to an end. You'd think that what happens on the Christmas do should stay on the Christmas do; but this is the twenty-first century, readers, and where would we be without social-networking sites to share the pictures of our annual works night out with other colleagues, friends, relations and the rest of cyberspace!

My father used to say to me, readers, "Never bet on anything unless you are absolutely certain." Well, readers, I'm going to bet you something, and I know that it's a sure-fire certainty.

Imagine you have driven past a restaurant and thought to yourself, 'That would be a nice place to take the missus for an evening out,' and in no time at all you have found yourself flicking through the Yellow Pages in search of the phone number. A quick call later and a table for two is booked for Saturday night at eight o'clock.

Saturday comes. You've had a good day. You've got out of the shopping trip to Sainsbury's; your team just won 4–0 at home to go third in the table; and at just gone half past seven your missus comes down the stairs looking stunning in a new dress which she swears blind she bought ages ago. It's going to be a good night because this restaurant does the best food for miles and is only one step away from a Michelin star.

The taxi arrives on time – you leave the car at home because you fancy a drinkie-poo or two – and you walk into the restaurant. The immaculately dressed maître d' welcomes you and shows you to your table. Menus and wine lists abound and you can imagine it taking all night to order just because of the ultra-yummy things that are on the menu. After much discussion with the missus, and a chat with the waiter, you order, and it's now that you become aware of something around you being not quite right.

Within ten feet of where you are sitting, ready to embark on your romantic dinner for two, there is another couple, as well dressed as you and your good lady. They are eating their first course in total silence. This, then, is my bet with you, readers. In fact, it isn't really a bet; it's more a cast-iron guarantee. To begin with the silence seems funny and you begin to wonder if it's your imagination, so to confirm that you are not going mad or sitting in a library you draw the attention of your missus to the silent partners. After funny, it becomes strange, then weird and finally unnerving. The two of them sit there in silence for the whole meal – all three courses and a coffee afterwards. Between courses they both stare into space. Not one single word is spoken between them! Mr Silent Partner finally attracts the attention of the waiter, and the bill is delivered to their table and paid. Finally they both get up and leave, and still not one single word is spoken between them. I'm guessing that one of them must have suggested going out, and they both dressed up to the nines almost as if they were going to the Palladium, so why then have they just sat through an excellent meal – and it was an excellent meal, I might stress – in total silence? I can promise you, readers, that the next time you go out for a 'posh nosh' meal they will be there, almost within punching range. Of course it isn't always like that. On another occasion another silent couple didn't speak for almost an entire meal, until midway through their last course of cheese and biscuits, when the lady suddenly leant forward and said in a low voice, "Of course, you know, I can't stand to watch people cut bread left-handed." It came from out of nowhere and failed to generate a response from her husband. Judging by the look on his face, he was mulling over her statement for the rest of the evening – in fact he probably still is; and I've never got to the bottom of it either.

You also get the other end of the scale – the non-stop chatterers. Although I've known this to go wrong on occasion, once a couple next to me chatted throughout their meal, but the lady didn't eat a single thing she had in front of her. The man had no such qualms and wolfed his steak and chips in record time. Very strange! For me, trying to eat a meal whilst sitting in the company of two people who look for all the world as though they ought to be plugged into the electric is distinctly discomforting.

Now don't get me wrong: I'm sorry if I've given the impression that I don't like going out for a meal, because that most definitely is not the case. Most restaurants give good service, with great food and a pleasant atmosphere; but when it isn't like that, I instantly get the impression that something out of the ordinary is transpiring. Having a wandering curiosity (all right, all right, a downright nosy streak), I am soon peering across at the plates of my fellow diners. The restaurants referred to in this chapter, readers, are your bog-standard restaurants – ones you could stumble across any time, anywhere.

This is not the end of the subject; there's more in the next chapter, so please read on – if you dare.

Oh yes, and the next time you're down the chippie with a large order of just about everything with chips, have a look over your shoulder as you near the counter. That shabby, bedraggled bloke standing just inside the door – it's me!

Chapter 6

Checking Out, Checking In

Checking in and staying at a hotel, whether it be for only one night, for a long weekend or even for a whole week has given me, readers, some of the most head-shakingly unbelievable, downright strange and curiously weird moments of all my world-watching experiences. In fact, I'm pretty sure that it's hotels where all my world-watching began!

There isn't much to say about checking into a hotel. There isn't normally a queue of other checker-inners, and beyond the receptionist trying to give you a different room from the one you asked for (for example, a view of the bins out the back rather than a vista of the bay out the front) what could go wrong? In fact, I can't remember ever having any trouble checking into a hotel anywhere in the world. However, there is one incident at a hotel reception that will always remain in my memory. After a day's excursioning round the local sights, I arrived back at my hotel at about half past five in the afternoon. Needing to ask at reception about the opening times of something, I stood behind a lady that had just arrived.

She was dressed very 'tweedily' – tweed suit and hat and brogues. She looked like something out of the late-Victorian/ early-Edwardian era – almost as if she'd booked a hunting lodge on the Balmoral Estate rather than coming for a seaside holiday in July on the south coast. She had a multitude of suitcases – seven to be exact – none of them matching, and all different shapes and sizes. She had already checked in, and now she was giving the two women on reception a blow-by-blow account of her journey from her (no doubt) seven-bedroomed town house in London to here at the Buena Vista Hotel at Pebbly Beach-on-Sea. The tale itself wasn't that memorable, but the delivery and the accent on the letter H was astounding.

"Hoh, do you know, hi have had a nightmare hof a journey. Hi had to come hon the Hem-25 hand then via the Hay-30. Hi was going to call hin hon my daughter-hin-law, but was running so very late; now hi shan't see her till Haugust."

She spoke in such a way that you found yourself holding your breath. A glimpse over her shoulder alerted her to my presence, and this curtailed her H-ridden story; but this wasn't the end of her. I saw her again later that evening in the restaurant, sitting at table eight (or should that be height, pronounced hate?). She then (h)ordered her food and made a point that she didn't want much to eat.

"Can hi just have hay three-hegg homelette hand French fries, please?" she said finally.

After eating it she disappeared into the night, and that was the last I saw (or heard) of her.

In my life I had never before heard the letter H so overused that no word in the English language began with a vowel, though I had come across other examples. Once I told an extremely posh lady who lived in the big house on the hill up the road that I was unable to take her payment over the phone. I said she would have to go on to our website to pay, whereupon she exclaimed in a high-pitched awfully posh Roedean-y accent, "Hoh, hi don't do honline!"

Relating this story straight after I put the phone down caused much hilarity in the office, and the story and catchphrase to this day are fondly told to anyone who'll listen.

The only other time was at a quiz night. After eight rounds, two teams were tied on the same number of points and a tiebreaker question was required to decide the outright winner.

The question was asked by the quizmaster and the first team captain to shout out the correct answer won first prize. The question was "Name Britain's only poisonous snake."

The lady team captain on Table 3 had the answer: "Hoh, that's hay hadder!" she exclaimed, raising one arm and half rising out of her seat.

Gawd alone knows what Henry Higgins would make of it all!

So, readers, we've checked in, unpacked, had a quick snooze and freshened up and now it's time to head down to dinner to sample the local fare.

One particular hotel dinner was unforgettable – not for the food, but for the company of the couple on the adjacent table. It was a small hotel on the Isle of Wight, and the restaurant wasn't particularly large. By the time we'd arrived the only table left was at the far end, where the room narrowed to a point. The walls were all glass, so a nice view of the sea and boats was in front of us both, even though we were sitting opposite each other. This, though, was to pass us by completely because of the discussion between the fifty-something-year-old couple on the table next to us. Their first course passed without incident; it was midway through their 'mains' that it all started. Previously they had been talking in hushed tones, but now an increase in decibels came in.

"Yes, I have!" he exclaimed in a loud voice out of nowhere. I'm guessing that at this point she contradicted him, because he exclaimed, "Yes, I have!" again, five decibels louder. Dropping back down to the previous level, he then firmly stated that he had indeed sailed his boat all the way to Plymouth; and not only that, but he'd done so on more than one occasion.

This time the sailor's wife's contradiction could be heard: "I don't know why it is that you feel you have to make up these stories. You've never been to Plymouth and certainly never sailed the boat that far. Do you know how far that is – Plymouth? Huh?"

He retorted with "I'm telling you, I have. I have sailed it that far and [ready for this?] you ought to know because you were on the boat with me."

"But I've never been to Plymouth and, I'm telling you this, there's no way I'd go that far on a boat, especially with you sailing it."

Silence now reigned. The rest of the main course, dessert and coffees and mints was eaten in look-down-at-the-table silence. I can't honestly say what was the more funny, the heated conversation or the looks now on their faces. They finished and left before we did, but not by much.

When we left, as I passed the maître d' I felt it was only right and proper to thank her for the meal, and for the entertainment. "Oh, my God!" she shrieked. "What was all that about?" I opened my mouth, but before I could speak she said, "Hold on. Hold on. Sally was serving them. Wait until she comes back." Our waitress had now arrived, and Sally arrived a few minutes later. "Right, go on," The maître d' said expectedly, and I had to tell them the whole sorry tale of how Mrs Francis Drake hadn't believed in, or had been part of, her husband's race to the Tamar Estuary on more than one occasion.

"Well, we wondered what on earth had happened. I'm so sorry it ruined your meal," she said, wringing her hands.

"No, not at all," I said, walking away. "I haven't been to the Isle of Wight for years; I'd forgotten it was this much fun."

The next two stories happened a few years apart. On each occasion my mother and I were having our evening meal alone together, the two of us having gone away for a few days. It was probably a significant birthday or Mother's Day. Both stories have incredible entertainment value.

The first story starts in a hotel restaurant. We'd arrived and been directed to the table that matched our room numbers. We perused the menus and placed our orders for our starters and main courses. Whilst waiting for our prawn cocktails to turn up we compared notes on what we had or didn't have in our rooms.

Two couples arrived and sat at a table for four about ten feet from us. There's nothing special about that. One couple were a husband and wife in their late thirties, and the other couple were probably in their late sixties. I'm guessing here, but I think the older couple were the parents of the younger woman. The older woman did bear a remarkable similarity to the younger one.

The restaurant was very nouveau cuisine, so basically we weren't going to get much for our money; but the food was very nice. The two couples managed to order – no problem. They ate their starter – no problem. The younger husband, faced with a magical menu of delights, then decided to have steak. The steak came with a mushroom-sauce garnish, which came in a little sauce boat. He held it like a hand-warmer and not by the handle, peering at it for several seconds before showing it to his wife, then to his mother-in-law and finally to his uninterested father-in-law. After a whispered discussion between them, Mrs Wife made a decision. She didn't wait for the waitress to come back. Oh no, she went over and stood outside the kitchen doors, ready to nab the next poor unsuspecting soul who should come through them. It was a young waitress and an animated discussion immediately ensued. Clearly the young waitress was unable to make a decision regarding the wife's request, so a senior waitress came over to see what was occurring. Mrs Senior Waitress made a decision and Mrs Wife returned to the table. We soon discovered what the request was: a side order of chips! Mr Husband was delighted with his acquisition; Mrs Wife wasn't, though. Back she went to her regular spot, hanging round outside the kitchen doors. This time it was a waiter whom she accosted. She made a request and returned to her seat. Her second request soon turned up: it was a large dish containing – wait for it – tomato ketchup. All four of them then proceeded to take turns, picking up a chip and dipping it into the ketchup in a perfect greasy-spoon-type manner. Now, don't get me wrong, readers – there's absolutely nothing wrong with greasy spoons and transport cafés. I love 'em, but come on – when in Rome . . . !

There's more. Mrs Wife had elected to have the crab. It was served as it should be, in its shell, but that isn't how she decided to eat it. She proceeded to hold the poor crab at least twelve inches up in the air in her right hand, and forked the contents out with her left hand so that they tumbled on to her plate like a mini crabmeat Niagara Falls. Then, when I thought it couldn't get any worse, three mouthfuls in she started choking. Now there is choking and there is choking to death; this choking was done in the most affected and dramatic way possible. Waiters and waitresses descended from all four corners of the restaurant clutching large jugs of water. Hopes that I had that they were going to throw the water over the woman were dashed; instead they poured her out a large glass, but with such speed and incompetence that the ice cubes and slice of lemon in the jug shot out and bounced across the table between her mother and father and fell on to the floor behind them. The offending piece of crabmeat was soon dislodged, but I was by now at the stage where I couldn't decide whether to laugh or cry. In fact, I was actually doing both and I'm sorry, readers, but I just had to leave them to it!

My second tale of a mother-shared dinner was again during a stay in a hotel, but this time we didn't use the restaurant. Instead we went to a nice cosy country pub complete with a log fire, exposed beams and horse brasses hanging off the walls. Having found a nice table of our own choosing, and having placed our order at the food counter at the draughty end of the bar, we sat down and waited for our starter to appear. The restaurant section of this pub wasn't exactly what you might call full, so it was a bit of a surprise when a group of people came in and parked themselves at a table immediately adjacent to ours. They consisted of a man dressed very much like Mr Toad, although not quite as rotund; a woman dressed in what can only be described as a flapper dress from the twenties, complete with a feather in her hair and a long string of pearls; and their four daughters, who all looked the spitting image of one another, dressed identically, but clearly of different ages as they were all of different heights. It seemed that the eldest daughter was celebrating her birthday, and the look on her face suggested that she was having to do the 'parent thing' that night, it being Friday. Perhaps she was able to go out with all her friends on the following night. A low-voiced discussion followed on what they were all going to have to eat and drink. Once they had ordered, they were told the food would take a while as there were several orders in front of theirs, ours included. The family started talking amongst themselves – but not for long. You know when you visit a friend in hospital and the conversation dries up within five minutes once you've got beyond the "Well, how are you getting on?" stage, but you feel you should stay for an hour out of some sense of duty – well, it was a bit like that. So, with all conversation dried up, Mr Toad decided to 'do the presents'.

"Georgair, Georgair, this one is from me and Mummair, me and Mummair," he proclaimed in a beautifully pruned Home Counties accent.

I couldn't stretch my neck far enough to see whether it was a wristwatch or a bracelet.

Several other gifts were handed out, but our food had turned up and, rather than watching, I was busy tucking in to my chicken New Yorker and chips. I was aware, though, that straight after the present-giving the conversation had dried up again. However, Mr Toad's half a lager shandy was now beginning to take effect.

He broke the silence: "Anyone know any jokes?"

His question met with blank faces, curled bottom lips and head-shaking.

He tried again: "Come on, girls – you must know at least one."

The deafening silence continued.

"Well, I have one. Do you want to hear it? Would you like to hear it?"

The resigned looks on their faces told me they knew they were going to hear it anyway. No one answered.

This, then, is the joke he told. I must emphasise, readers, just how strong his awfully posh accent was, how sharp every vowel was and how every consonant was strangled to death. Here goes:

"This chap and his wife go riding every Sunday, without fail, winter and summer. However, on this particular Sunday she has a very bad cold and doesn't even get out of bed.

"'Are you not coming today, darling?'

"She shakes her head.

"'Oh, that's a shame. I will have to go on my own, then.'

"When he arrives at the stables he wanders over to the tack room, where he meets the groom.

"'Your wife not with you today, sir?' he says.

"'No, no – on my own today. She has influenza.'

"The groom asks the chap to pass on his good wishes and says he hopes she'll be OK for next Sunday.

"As they part, the chap takes down what he thinks is his saddle only for the groom to put him straight: 'No, that isn't your saddle, sir. That's your wife's.'

"'How do you know?' the chap asks, amazed that the groom could tell the difference.

"'Because', the groom states, 'she has a problem putting it on the horse, and that's why she has "Right" on one side and "Left" on the other.'

"'Oh!' exclaims this chap, 'that explains why then she has "C&A" on her knickers.'"!

I thought I was going to either choke on my chicken or be sick. The joke itself is funny, especially with the voice and accent it was told in, but it struck me as hysterical because of the fact that he'd told it in the company of his wife and four daughters. Nobody laughed, except me; but I managed to stifle the laugh as I didn't want him to see that I'd been earwigging his joke.

His wife's reaction said it all: "Fred! I can't believe you just said that."

Fred was a picture of innocence. "What? I don't think it was that bad," he said, disappointed that his joke hadn't met with a standing ovation.

My mother leant forward in her seat and whispered to me, "I don't get it," with the result that I had to stifle my laughter a second time; and I had to make her a promise that I would try to explain it to her later – which I did.

Just for younger readers I think I'd better explain that C&A was a nationwide clothing department store way back in the mists of time – well, not that many mists, but a while back anyway.

It was at about this time that the family's dinners turned up, and not a word was spoken or even a sound heard from them for the rest of the evening. They actually left before we did.

Their leaving spurred my mother into life. She pressed me for an explanation and I had to retell the joke there and then. She's got it now!

Let's have a recap. You've arrived at your hotel, found your room, unpacked and been fed and watered. You're now back in your room and ready for a restful night's sleep after your long journey, in readiness for the day of sightseeing ahead of you tomorrow. What could go wrong? It's a Saturday, and what's the betting that there is a party going on downstairs in the bar, which has been especially booked and fitted out for the occasion? I wonder why it is that at stag dos they always play Andy Williams singing 'Can't Take My Eyes off You', and all the well-oiled blokes in attendance find themselves mumbling their way through the lyrics – that is until they get to the 'I love you, baby' bit, which is yelled out at 100 decibels, having been preceded by the 'dur-dur, dur-dur, dur-dur, dur-dur, durrrr' bit! Also, how come at hen dos you can always guarantee that one of the girls ends up crying? And guess whose door she finds herself slumped against and crying outside of? Yes, that's the one! Obviously her bum did look too big in it and her so-called best friend, after a few Martinis and tequila slammers, has informed her of the fact.

Then there's always the dreaded twenty-first birthday party. If you had a bottom dollar, you could bet it on the chance that they will play 'The Birdie Song' – and not just once, but for half the night. You don't have to see them doing the actions; you can picture them doing them with your eyes closed. That's actually eyes closed, under the duvet and your head buried between the two pillows to drown out the noise.

At last the party breaks up and peace rules. Not a chance! Some of the party have elected to stay the night – or, rather, what's left of it – in the hotel, and the next hour or so is spent with several knocks at my door and shouts of "Are you in there, Tim? Tim, are you in there?"

A fellow partygoer, slightly less inebriated, usually puts them straight with a "No, he's in 36; that's 32."

Another knock at the door is followed this time with a "Sorry, mate – got the wrong room!"

You don't say!

Once again, all is quiet – but not for long. You think you can hear voices in the corridor, but actually it's only one voice. One of the partygoers is having to report in to his girlfriend that he is OK and has had a great evening. This involves him wandering up and down the corridor on his mobile phone, having the most utterly pointless conversation when one text should have been enough. Having confirmed with her seventy-eight times that he's OK, and sixty-four times that he has had a great evening, after twenty-five minutes of nocturnal corridor wanderings he finally calls it a day and goes back to his room.

All is quiet now, readers, and it's three o'clock in the morning. All hope of any sleep is long gone.

Bleary-eyed you emerge from your room at five to nine. They only serve breakfast until nine, so there has to be a race downstairs to the dining room if you want to get any breakfast. Aha, breakfast – the best meal of the day, don't they say? Quite right too! There is no question that the full English breakfast is the best breakfast in the world. No one can match the English for the myriad of items that have been sneaked over the years on to the traditional English breakfast menu.

Somehow, when people come down for breakfast all common sense seems to fly out the window. The difficulty they have in ordering scrambled eggs and bacon – it's almost as if they have had a frontal lobotomy at some point during the night. Their very arrival in the dining room seems to daunt them. It never ceases to amaze me that so many people don't just sit down, but instead look around them as if they don't know what tables and chairs are for.

The best (or worst, depending on your point of view) example of this I ever saw took place whilst I was munching on my extra toast, having just had scrambled eggs and bacon. Six people wandered in and stood like refugees that had just crossed the border into a neighbouring country. They seemed to be wondering where they should go now. All six stood looking in different directions, as if in the hope of finding somewhere to sit in an almost totally deserted dining room. There was only me and an elderly couple sucking on their grapefruit segments. After a minute or two of this they seemed to agree on a table a few feet from them, but they continued to stand hexagonally. Finally a waitress appeared and was cornered by the hungry half-dozen.

"Excuse me. There's six of us. Do we sit at the table that's been set up for six?" one of them said whilst clutching the waitress's arm with his right hand and gesticulating with his left at the table they'd earmarked.

Her reply was delivered in the most gravelly Belfast accent I had ever heard. She sounded a bit like an irritated Ian Paisley. "Haven't you been for breakfast before?" she asked.

"Oh, yes, this is our third day here," one of the men replied, helpfully.

"Well, yes, then" came her reply, equally gravelly and irritated, but this time with a large dollop of sarcasm to go with it.

The six trooped over to the table, which was clearly theirs all along, and proceeded to eat their breakfast in mortified silence.

A few years ago someone came up with the concept of having the first course at breakfast as a self-service feature, with the result that nowadays you often have to help yourself if you want fruit juice, tea, coffee or a dish of snap-and-crackly wheaty flakes. The idea was slow to catch on, but is now becoming quite regular everywhere you go. It is very helpful if you want to catch the early train home.

I saw an abuse of this system a couple of years ago when a chap in his late twenties went up for a glass of orange juice. He had to queue, as the person currently in charge of the orange-juice pitcher was none other than yours truly. Once I had finished I offered him the jug. This confused him completely, so I put it back down on the 'starter table', only for him to pick it up and pour himself a large glass. We both went back to our tables and sat down. I had only taken a sip from mine when I noticed him going back to the 'starter table' with his empty glass. He filled it up again, walked back to his table, sat down, drank it in two gulps, got up, walked back to the 'starter table', poured himself a third glass, walked back to his table, sat down, drank it, got up, walked back to the 'starter table', poured himself a fourth glass, walked back to his table, sat down, drank it . . . Do I need to go on, readers? I have never in my life seen anyone drink so much orange juice.

When the waitress came out of the kitchen clutching a large full English breakfast she walked past the 'starter table'. After delivering the breakfast to an elderly gent, she returned the same way she had come and glanced at the, by now, almost empty jug. She momentarily stopped as she did a double take at the depleted receptacle. She took it with her back to the kitchen and reappeared several minutes later with it filled to the brim. She placed it on the 'starter table' and went back to the kitchen. No sooner had she gone than the whole rigmarole started up again. I have no idea how many glasses he had (I lost count at seven), but I do know that he was still guzzling after I'd left the dining room. Even the Man from Del Monte, in all his years travelling the world for the best fruit, couldn't have drunk this much!

Another great up-and-down breakfast happened a few months after this at the same hotel. A young man had come in after me, found a table and sat down. He obviously didn't know the 'starter table' system, so he sat with his hands placed in his lap, staring into space. The waitress arrived and asked what he wanted, and after a minute or two's discussion she took the order and pointed her pen at the collection of juices and cereals as she walked away. The young man got up from his seat and poured himself an orange juice, sat back down and sipped it gingerly – well, more slurped than sipped actually. Having taken only one mouthful, he then got up from his seat again, this time to go the unisex toilet, which was located just outside the dining room. On arriving back, he sat down, then got up and headed over to the 'starter table' again, this time for a cup of coffee. He walked back to his table, sat down, took a slurp of the coffee and sat back in his seat, staring into space again. It was then as if a light had been switched on. He jumped up from his seat and disappeared out of the dining room. He was gone for several minutes, during which time his breakfast turned up – and the full works it was too, with extra bacon. The waitress looked around, puzzled, as she put the plate down, and she looked at me for an explanation. I replied to her glance with a combination of raised eyebrows and shrugged shoulders. Suddenly, he reappeared just as she was going back to the kitchen, in time to thank her for delivering his breakfast. There was a newsagent's across the road from the hotel and he must have popped across for a copy of the *Daily Mirror*, which he proceeded to place on the floor at his feet.

With everything in place, he now tackled his breakfast. No, I don't mean he started to eat it; I mean he *attacked* it. Every item – bacon, fried egg, sausage, tomato and mushroom – was ruthlessly hacked at, and not one piece of it did he actually eat! He did eat his toast, though – just one of the two slices he'd been given. I watched in disbelief as he spread the butter on this one slice with the bowl of his spoon – yes, readers, his *spoon*. He then ate it so fast it was as if his life depended upon it, got up out of his seat and left the dining room, and the *Daily Mirror*, all in the space of two minutes.

I'd finished, and with a look of "Just what was all that about?" on my face, I got up and left the dining room too, but not before I met the waitress coming back out from the kitchen. I thanked her for the breakfast and, of course, for the entertainment (not the first time I've done that, readers – see above), and enquired if I had to pay her separately for it, or could I add it to my bill when I checked out? Do you know what she said to me? She said, "Just what was all that about?" I gave her a brief synopsis of what she had missed whilst hiding in the kitchen, but I don't think she had any more of an idea than I had – or indeed you have, readers.

My last breakfast tale took place at a hotel in Cornwall a few years ago. It was one of those hotels that welcome coach parties, although this was unknown to me when I booked – and, indeed, when I went down for breakfast on my first morning. The first I knew of it was when I took my seat next to the window in the dining room. I'm partial to a sea view when I'm eating my bacon and eggs, and as I gazed out of the window I saw a coach parked on the other side of the road. The only sign of human life was a sweating and clearly out-of-breath chap struggling back and forth across the road from the hotel with three or four suitcases at a time and loading them into the underneath storage part of the coach. The coach itself was empty of people, and, oddly enough, so was the dining room I was sitting in. I was just starting to think that perhaps there was another restaurant when a waitress with an ear-to-ear smile came over, asked my room number and took my order. This was in the days before the 'starter table' system.

"Where is everyone?" I enquired.

"You're our only guest," she replied, "other than the coach party from Derby."

As soon as she had gone, and as I watched Mr Sweaty Driver carrying two large vermilion suitcases across the road, the peace and quiet of the sunny Cornish morning was disturbed. What started as a low rumbling increased until it sounded like an oncoming train as a great mass of people charged into the dining room.

I hadn't noticed it before, but a large number of tables had been put together in an L shape. The coach party took every seat. There were about fifty of them and not one was under seventy; also the split was about right for a group of that age – i.e., six men to forty-four women!

Three waitresses appeared and took their breakfast orders. This was done fairly easily, with no fuss, but the non-stop chattering, which sounded like four dozen pneumatic drills, went on right through the order-taking and while I ate my hash browns and wholemeal toast.

While I was sipping my coffee, their breakfast orders came out, and that's when the trouble started. Clutching two huge plates of breakfast, waitress number one shouted out the contents of the plate in her left hand: "Two fried eggs, bacon 'n' sausages."

71

No response.

She tried it again: "Two fried eggs, bacon 'n' sausages."

The chattering stopped and silence descended.

A slight murmuring started up and then one voice was heard: "Didn't you order that, Lily?"

Lily, several seats away from the voice, responded with an "Eh?"

"Didn't you order two fried eggs, bacon 'n' sausages?"

Lily thought for a second. "No, that wasn't what I ordered."

Waitress number one tried it again: "Two fried eggs, bacon 'n' sausages."

No response.

The look on her face suggested that she wanted to be somewhere else – it mattered not where, just somewhere else.

"Hang on," said Lily. "Did you say two fried eggs, bacon 'n' sausages?"

"I did," replied waitress number one, sighing slightly.

"Oh, well, yes, then, that's me," said Lily.

Waitress number one placed the now partially cold and congealing eggs in front of Lily. We were off and running – one down; forty-nine to go.

Waitresses two and three had by now arrived, and were standing, plate in each hand like two bookends, shouting out the contents of their plates like two costers selling their wares at a London market. I munched my way through four slices of toast – well, I was hungry, readers – and in that time only eight breakfasts were put out. Each order was met with blank expressions and an en-masse discussion. And so it went on.

My breakfast finished, I left the dining room, thanked my waitress, who was clearly not in the mood for conversation, and went back to my room. I came back down the stairs half an hour later and passed the dining-room door. They were still in there and the chattering had increased in volume. Shooting a glance inside I saw a waitress coming out with two breakfasts from the kitchen.

I didn't hear what she said the orders were, but I swear I heard someone say, "Didn't you order that, Lily?"

Leaving the hotel, I spotted the coach driver leaning against the front of his coach, still sweating and having a fag. He'd finished loading.

I proffered a "Good morning."

He gave me an acknowledgement by a nodding of his head and a raising of his eyebrows, but the look on his face did not suggest that he was looking forward to the day ahead.

"We're off to Padstow for lunch," he said grumpily.

"Good luck with that," was my half-smiling, half-sniggering reply.

He looked puzzled at my response, but I didn't hang around to continue the conversation.

Finally, then, you're at the end of your stay. Bags have been repacked and, after a quick shufti round the room to make sure you've not left the toothbrush under the bed, it's time to head off to reception and check out.

Apart from having to queue behind an entire cricket team who were on tour, and having to wait for almost an hour for my turn, I can honestly say that I have never had many problems checking out of a hotel. One incident that does spring to mind happened when I arrived at reception to find a lady checking out clutching a small overnight case, a large purple hatbox and a Yorkshire terrier. There was a heated discussion going on about some of the extras that had appeared on her bill.

"Yes, I did use the telephone, but there was no way that I was on the phone for any length of time, so it can't be that much," she said most indignantly. "And I didn't order any food in my room; I just asked for a bowl so that Figgy[!] could have his dinner. Surely you are not going to charge me for that?"

After a few inaudible mutterings by the receptionist, and a firm "I will have to ask the manager," she disappeared, only to reappear five minutes later with the same bill, now with several crossings-out and a revised total at the bottom.

Mrs Yorkie Terrier was happy to pay now, and a platinum card was produced. Having paid, she tottered off in the direction of the main door, at one point dropping the hatbox and nearly dropping the case, but at all times making sure she clung on to Figgy tightly.

"I bet you get to see it all in here," I said to the receptionist once the lady had gone, trying to make light of the situation.

"It's always like that," she replied. "She's a regular and questions her bill every time she stays here."

Owing to the harassed look on the receptionist's face, I decided not to do as I'd planned, which was to book a future date at the hotel; I just paid up and left.

Outside I ran into Mrs Yorkie Terrier again. She was trying to bundle her three items into the back of a taxi. I very briefly considered asking her if she required any assistance, but Figgy started yapping; so, deciding that discretion was the better part and all that, I headed off to catch my train.

They say we are all different, and in my experience nowhere is this more apparent than when we are staying in a hotel. Ask any hotel employee and they will tell you there is no such thing as your average guest. I cannot believe that Joe Public, regardless of age or sex, behaves in his normal day-to-day life or in his own home like he does in a hotel. All I can say is I'm pleased that it's so. Like I said at the start of this chapter, hotels are where it all began for me; so, for all those people that have ever signed a hotel register and then eaten their dinner or breakfast within earshot or in sight of me, I thank you. Never in the field of human tourism was so much owed to so many by one person.

Chapter 7

The Pride and the Passion

As with most blokes, I do have a passion for sport. Through the years I have had an interest, at some point, in almost every well-known sport. My enthusiasm for sport comes from my father – after all, he did finish top of the bowling averages for our town at the age of fifty. He was very much a cricket-in-the-summer-and-football-in-the-winter kind o' guy, and, like me, he was interested in other sports too. However, he never liked motor racing, although he always claimed that he could have been a great speedway rider. He used to take me out into the back garden to kick a football or wave a cricket bat at almost every opportunity he got – just after I started walking, probably. I don't remember any quarter being given either!

The first football match he ever took me to was when I was eight years old, although my interest in football had started long before that. Our town was geographically placed a long way from any 'big' clubs, so the only league club I was taken to was Gillingham, and that was the way it remained on and off for the next thirty years until I finally stopped supporting them. In those days, of course, there wasn't the football coverage that we get nowadays. We had to make do with *Match of the Day* on Saturday nights and *The Big Match* on Sunday afternoons after lunch. But the one thing that has never changed is the magical word you often hear: atmosphere. Anyone that goes regularly to a football match will know what I am talking about, but to those who unfortunately only watch on a TV I will try my best to explain it. I have often got into arguments about whether someone is a supporter of a football club or only a follower.

"Who do you support?"

"I support Liverpool and have done for twenty years" comes the proud reply.

"Oh, how often do you see them play?" I tend to ask.

"Oh, I don't – I just watch them when they come on the tele" – stated firmly and equally proudly.

"Oh, so you don't support them, then; you only follow them" is how I usually end the conversation – and, trust me, the conversation *does* end at that point.

To my mind, if you support your team, then you do, through thick and thin, no matter what. Supporting them means sitting in a freezing-cold stand, sleety snow blowing in your face, your extremities frost-bitten, shivering so much that you can't hold the programme let alone read the notes – and this is before kick-off. You then emerge at five o'clock looking like you've been following in the footsteps of Shackleton, having spent the last two hours watching your team lose 4–0. Then the following week you go through it all again – not sitting cosily on the settee with a beer or two and a pizza. And all too often when you see a match on the TV you know the result already.

Sorry, readers – now see what you've done! I'm getting on my soapbox now!

The first day of a new season is usually played in eighty degrees of heat, and the end of the season can be quite balmy too, but it tends to be in the autumn and spring days that the atmosphere is at its best. It's not too cold and your team has settled into a rhythm by October; by March you can usually see where the season is headed, and from about this time the regular songs are sung more frequently and the new songs (introduced this season) are getting louder and being put across more vehemently. The referee's parentage will always be called into question along with what he likes to spend his spare time doing.

The true fan will never call the linesman a referee's assistant, but he is often called 'lino', as in "Come on, lino – keep up with the play", when another almost certain offside is missed by the flag-waver.

All this has distracted me from what I wanted to tell you. It's not those moments out there on the pitch, but those in the stands or on the terraces that made going to the game the experience it was.

One particular game that never got going was enlivened about ten minutes before half-time when a young lady, probably about nineteen or twenty years old, walked past the front of the stand on her way, no doubt, to the hot-dog stand. I say 'no doubt' as she was carrying in her hand a large plastic bag full of burger buns for the half-time cheeseburgers.

Someone recognised her and from twenty rows back yelled out, "Katie!" whereupon 'Katie' waved back in the voice's direction whilst holding in the same hand the cumbersome bag of buns.

This prompted a second voice to call out, "Nice baps, love!" much to the hilarity of the rest of the stand.

Katie, meanwhile, had quickened her pace, no doubt to hide her embarrassment.

The chap sitting next to me leant forward and said so that only I could hear it, "Betcha don't get that at Old Trafford!"

I smiled and nodded in agreement.

A near riot nearly broke out once when a chap in the same row as me took a photograph of a player (he had once been very famous but had fallen down the leagues in his football dotage) when he came over to our side of the ground to take a throw-in. Before I knew it, two stewards appeared from nowhere, and it was almost as if it had been an assassination attempt the way they pounced on him.

"Ya not allowed to take photos of the game, mate," steward number one said gruffly as steward number two was grabbing the budding David Bailey's right arm in an attempt to eject him from the stadium. Thankfully, a chap in the row in front spoke up for him, saying, "He was taking a picture of me – he's always taking pictures of me. He's got an album full of them at home." The two stewards now stood perplexed and with a 'we will have to take your word for it' kind of attitude slouched back to their seats, glowering at the crowd.

Now, I'm not religious. I think, readers, that you may have already gathered that, but I admit to praying at football matches on many occasions and I have even joined in the community singing of some quite famous hymns (although the words have been changed to fit the occasion more suitably). I always love the one voice that sings in echo to everybody else. Five hundred people sing the first line and then one person sings the same line before the 500 sing the second line. It's called atmosphere, folks, and you don't get it watching the TV! Sorry – soapboxing again!

The one thing at a football match that gets me above all others is when less than fifteen minutes into a game people have an uncontrollable desire to get up and fetch a drink or something to eat. I just don't understand this.

At Wembley a few years back I had managed to get two tickets for me and my mate to see an England game. The tickets weren't cheap, but that didn't matter – I mean, how often do you get to see England at Wembley? Now, in fairness, this game was not one of England's best, but the entertainment from the almost non-stop human traffic that was getting up and walking from their seat during the game was astounding. One or two of them literally got up four or five times between kick-off and half-time, sometimes coming back with food, sometimes with a drink and sometimes empty-handed. Like me, they must have paid over £60 for a ticket, so you'd think they could sit for forty-five minutes until it was half-time before fetching a Coke! Don't get me wrong, I'm one of the first to jump up to celebrate a goal or to put my point across at some injustice or other, but I don't like having to stand up every five minutes or so, getting my toes trodden on in the process, just because someone can't wait twenty minutes for a hot dog with extra mustard. It is utterly beyond me.

I know it's not only me that picks up on it. Without fail at every home match an elderly chap would get up from his seat from about twelve rows back around thirty minutes into the game. He would then walk down the steps at the side of the stand and walk along the path in front of it accompanied by over 100 supporters standing up in their seats, arms outstretched, swaying gently from side to side as if they were piloting Lancaster Bomber, 'nur-nurring' 'The Dambusters March'.

Cricket too has its fair share of up-and-downers, but they can be excused, I suppose. It can be a long day sitting in the sun.

What better way to watch a cricket match than with a glass of cold beer in your hand! This brings us to a family incident that happened many years ago. It took place at The Oval on the first day of the last test in the year that has been designated ever since as Botham's Ashes. My sister had managed to get four tickets for us, my mother and father included. It was a warm day towards the end of August and four gents further along our row were stripped to the waist, each taking it in turn to get the beers in. Finally it was this chap's turn and the several pints he had had already were starting to take effect. We all shuffled back in our seats to let him squeeze past, but it was when he came back with his tray of four pints of lager that the trouble started. Having edged past my father and then me, he attempted the same movement past my sister, who had moved her summery open-toed sandals to the right and towards me to avoid them being trodden on. This chap, concentrating like mad on his four pints so as not to spill any more than he had already, and with general alcohol-induced unsteadiness, lurched sideways, plonking his left foot down firmly on my sister's exposed big toe.

This caused her to exclaim, "Ow!" in a very loud voice, and in the same movement she directed a straight left punch which landed somewhere in the region of this chap's left kidney. And all this was going on right in the middle of Dennis Lillee's run up.

The poor bloke stood there in disbelief for a couple of seconds, whilst my mother on the other side curled up with embarrassment. How he held on to his beer I will never know – but he did, and without saying a word and with composure regained he set off along the row back to his colleagues.

My sister to this day is adamant that she moved her feet well out of the way and that he deserved it. However, the story still cannot be related at a family gathering without my mother firmly stating, "Oh, the embarrassment of it!"

The crowd at a cricket match are invariably well turned out, and the same can always be said of a horse-racing crowd. Racegoers are usually well dressed in a 'smart casual' way, and they are nearly always good-natured. Nothing normally kicks off, despite copious amounts of alcohol being consumed. The cacophony of sound that comes from a myriad of devotees (did you like that, readers) when their horse comes down the straight with a chance of winning is louder than any crowd at a football match when the home team have just scored the winning goal to beat their fiercest rivals. In fact, if you want to attend the sporting event with the best atmosphere, then without doubt the place to go is to a horse race. Royal Ascot is too packed and there it's an achievement just to get your bet on with the course bookie between races, so I will give you a helpful hint: try Sandown Park on Variety Club Day for a horsey day out. You may even get to rub shoulders with a few minor celebs, and the hog roast is always good too!

Have you ever noticed (and I think I'm aiming this more at indoor sportsmen than outdoor) the look of know-it-all smugness you get from gifted amateurs? Tenpin bowling is a good example of this. It doesn't matter when you go – any time day or night, during the week or at weekends – you can guarantee that one of the players in the lane next to you is utterly brilliant at tenpin bowling, and they make sure that they let you and everybody else know it. This sometimes happens playing snooker too, and, to a lesser extent, darts, but there is no question in my mind that if you book a lane at a bowling alley for an evening you will be treated to a display of tenpin bowling that you would otherwise only get as pay-per-view on Sky.

You feel quite pleased with yourself that you've suddenly managed to get a good technique going, and you've sent your ball off and it's fizzed down the lane and knocked over eight skittles. The little animation that flashes up on the scoreboard, depicting that you've got eight, matches your smile. Then what happens? Yep, master bowler next to you in Lane 6 flings his ball (and it probably is his own too!) so hard and fast that it looks set to break the land speed record. And then – and this is what gets me – he (or she) turns round nonchalantly, complete with a look of utter smugness, *before* the ball is halfway down the lane, *knowing* that all ten skittles will be smashed into oblivion and to all corners of the known universe. This is followed by high fives all round with his (or her) fellow competitors. This always happens within a few seconds of my getting my eight, and my lone two skittles momentarily look all forlorn until ten new ones are lowered into position in Lane 6. I'm willing to bet that the two which are left are one on either side, and I know I'm not going to hit either of them. And, sure enough, I don't. I also know that Mr/Mrs Smug Bowler sees that I haven't hit them.

Do you think I've got a hang-up about this, readers? Yes, I know I have, and it's made all the worse by the fact that Mr/Mrs Smug Bowler hasn't bowled another ball, but is still basking in the glory of the previous strike.

I send my next one down: eight again. It is as good as the previous one, but can you guess what comes next? Yep, ten skittles flying in all directions on Lane 6. This time the smug walk back is accompanied with a swaying of the hips – the walk and movement not all that dissimilar to that of a size-zero model on a Milan catwalk! More high fives follow. I find myself walking in little circles now, and I am contemplating that if they get overconfident on their next turn and only manage to knock down nine, I shall dash down the lane and find somewhere dark to put number ten!

I like going bowling – no, seriously, readers, I do – but the next time you're playing just have a quick shufti at the lane next to yours. There will be a world championship taking place; and if there isn't, then it will be going on in the next-but-one lane and between you and them will be standing a little bloke clutching a bowling ball with a look of murderous intent on his face. Yes, that will be me. Still, you have to admit it's a nice and fun way to spend an hour or two in the evening – I think!

When I was at school, one lad in my year was good at everything. You name it. Whether it was English, geography, physics, chasing girls, or athletics (it mattered not what it was), he was brilliant at it. And boy, didn't he know it! And boy, didn't he let everybody else know it too! He had the look of know-it-all smugness too, and a look of "Ain't I brilliant?" was never far from his face. This was a constant source of hilarity for us less studious types.

Athletics was his speciality, and every year on sports day he would break the corresponding year's record for whichever athletic event he condescended to enter.

We had another lad whose bag was table tennis. He wasn't in the same year as us ('us' being me and my card-playing mate from Chapter 2), but once a fortnight we would have games against the year below us, which included this Master Table Tenniser. He and his mate would play me and mine at doubles, and he always had an insane urge to thwack the ball at cannonball speed. Eight or nine times out of ten, the ball would ping off the edge of the table and bounce halfway across the sports hall, and the look of nonchalant smugness would spread across his one-of-those-faces-you-could-punch fizzog. Now, granted, I wasn't there for a half-hearted game of girlie ping-pong, but it would have been nice to have a game with a few rallies.

All players of racket sports, despite the fact that they are all open to the masses, have that 'OK, yah' and 'Hooray Henry' element about them, don't they? Whichever sport you decide to have a go at playing you either have the ability to shine at it or you haven't, but I think, readers, that my inability to play any sport with any great aplomb stems from being surrounded by smug show-offs who could throw, kick, hit and punch infinitely better than I ever could!

When I started this chapter I felt that participants and fans alike in all sports were fair game (sorry, readers – no pun intended) for my world-watching ways! I realise now that this is not the case.

Every sport has its own set of fans, and they are all very loyal to their chosen sport. They all say at some point, "Oh, it's not like the old days, you know." I'm like that with Formula One, and I find myself moaning on about the seemingly endless list of dos and don'ts that now exist. These days we have no flexibility of innovation (did you like that one too? I had to lie down for a minute or two when I thought of it) like we had in the sixties and seventies, but there I always am on a summer Sunday at one o'clock, ready for when the lights go out and the cars race down to the first corner.

If you are a fellow hardened (or should that be hard-nosed) devotee of any competitive sport, perhaps you will agree that we are even more committed to our chosen sport than the people taking part in it are. Perhaps you are one of those who spend hard-earned wages just to stand out in all weathers to cheer on your favourite team and players, in a division whose sponsors no one has ever heard of. You might also pay for and put up with public transport and the people on it(!) in order to get to the ground – not forgetting shelling out a vast fortune for the Panini stickers that go with any major sporting event. If you are such a fan, I salute you.

And, finally, I'm back to my favourite word for this chapter: atmosphere. The sport in question doesn't matter, but being there and yelling your lungs out does. The asides from your fellow lunatics and enthusiastic aficionados in the crowd, coupled with the little something that suddenly happens but was the last thing that you expected to happen and would never be seen on TV in a million years, makes it all worthwhile.

Chapter 8

A Last Look Round

When I started this book I (believe it or not, readers) had a rough idea of how and where it was going and I knew that the subjects covered in the seven previous chapters would furnish me with more than enough material. However, although I feel that I've probably put you through enough already, I wanted to include some anecdotes about a little bit of miscellaneous shufti-ing. To put it another way (as the bishop said to the actress), this chapter includes other occasions when odd out-of-the-blue incidents, however unbelievable, happened to yours truly. And unfortunately they still continue to happen.

I don't have the answer to life's little mysteries, but there are two things I staunchly believe in: one, that everything happens for a reason; and two, the thirty-second law. I'm going to have to explain the thirty-second law to you, readers, aren't I? It's very straightforward. It's when something out of the ordinary happens to you, and if you had just been thirty seconds earlier or later you wouldn't have experienced it – for instance, when a tree blows down in a gale just as a car is driving underneath it. If it had happened just thirty seconds later, or thirty seconds earlier, the accident wouldn't have happened. The wonder of this 'law' is that many things do actually happen in the thirty seconds before you arrive somewhere or thirty seconds after you've left. This chapter is all about the little things that, had I been a few seconds either side, I would not have been a witness to.

As good a subject to start with as any is supermarkets. No, I don't mean a small Co-op or a Tesco Express; I'm talking here about your lumping great, just slightly out-of-town hypermarket.

Let's start with your car in the car park. It matters not where you park your car, you can absolutely guarantee that someone within seconds will arrive in their car and will park it next to yours. The regularity with which this happens is astounding. I wish I could have a fiver for every time it did.

So having squeezed out of the door, because no doubt they parked too close to you, you collect your trolley and you are on your way to do the weekly, fortnightly or even monthly shop. I'll let you into a little secret, readers: the best time to go is between five and six in the afternoon on a Saturday. Why? Because it's a no-man's-land time. Most people either go on Friday night or Saturday morning. Some leave it until after lunch, but by that time in the early evening Joe Public is back indoors starting to get ready for an evening out or, at the very least, listening to the football results.

Anyway, you're in and they are all in there, everywhere you look: the ones that push the trolley with one hand, holding a list in the other; the ones that stop and start and make it up as they go along; and the ones that play hunter-gatherer, making a beeline for the meat counter first and then manhandling (or should that be 'person handling') the veggies as they make their way back down Aisle 9 looking for foam bathroom cleaner.

And, of course, there are always – how can I put this without sounding rude? – the town's more senior residents. Is there anyone out there in the cosmos that can please explain to me why it is that pensioners find it necessary to do their weekly shop on a Saturday afternoon? They literally have all week to do it. Everybody knows that Saturday afternoon is the busiest time of the week in a supermarket. Those that work Monday to Friday are there, and hordes of screaming brats are running around clutching blow-up models of a *T. rex*, yelling, "Mum, can I have this one?" or rolling round the floor in protest at having to go to the 'Back to School' section, where they are made to be a living mannequin whilst a pair of trousers is held up against them to see if they'll fit! So why, then? Why do senior residents come out and plod up and down the middle of the aisles, generally getting in the way of everybody, including the poor assistants having to restock on a Saturday afternoon when they could do it on, say, a Thursday morning with the whole place relatively deserted? Answers on a postcard, please!

There's a funny kind of protesting squeaking noise coming from the trolley at the weight of groceries and sundries piled high on it as you make your way to the checkout. I've always noticed that checkout assistants in supermarkets come in two types: those that are smily and chatty and those that look like their cat has just died. There is nothing in between.

You load your trolley contents on to the conveyor belt and wait patiently for your turn. Are you going to get a sunny "Hello" or a whatsthepointinliving.com deep-throated "Ug"? Either way, you or one of the people in front of you will not have a bar code, or, at least, not one that can be read by the scanner. The assistant's hand goes down below the counter and, from out of nowhere, a bell rings! I've never seen the bell, have you? Come to that, what else have they got hiding under there?

As if by magic, a supervisor appears, grabs the item and dashes off to the far end of the store. Have you noticed that they always come back with a firm announcement? "Them's £2.68." Then the whole production line starts up again.

We're done. The trolley's unloaded, everything's been through the scanner, and you've loaded up your biodegradable carrier bags and put them back in the trolley. Then you've put your card in and punched in the PIN number. Let's go!

No, you're not out yet! First you have to run the gauntlet of:

"Excuse me, sir, would you be interested in Warm 'n' Snugly double glazing?"

"Erm, no, thanks, I wouldn't."

"Are you sure, sir? We've got a good deal on at the moment: have fifteen windows fitted and get a sixteenth absolutely free."

"No, I'm not interested. Sorry." (What am I apologising for?)
"Well, take one of our leaflets in case you change your mind."
"OK. Thanks."

"Now that you've taken one of our leaflets, can I have your name, address, postcode, email address, mobile phone number and inside-leg measurement so that we can send you some more of our products."

"No! Argh!"

You dash towards the door with the trolley's protesting squeak going into overdrive.

At last you arrive back at the car to find that the car that arrived thirty seconds after you has gone. Now there's space all around you to unload your trolley – but not for long! With the whole car park to choose from, totally out of the blue a massive truck thing (a people carrier) roars up and parks next to you. You have to stop loading the boot and quickly shut the back door, which you had just opened two seconds previously so that you could throw your toilet rolls on to the back seat. Several kids come rolling out of this people carrier and your unloading has to stop until this sudden invasion has passed by.

It doesn't always happen like that. You sometimes get the alternative, which is that when you get back to the car and start unloading there is already a car parked next to yours. What happens is that the owners of that car come back at exactly the same time as you do and start unloading their trolley at the same time. Before you know it you end up banging trolleys and peering at what they've bought, or you find that you've flung the toilet rolls on to their back seat instead of yours! I can see why someone would want to invent online shopping, but come on – where's the fun in that?

Queuing at the checkout in a supermarket is always an experience, but then so is queuing generally. It seems to bring together a hotchpotch of human life that you would never normally see together, and this is probably why queuing is usually done in relative silence. The exception is, of course, when a woman yells to her husband and down my ear too, "D'ya fink we need any satsumas?"

I'm a terrible queue-jumper. I've been informed that if I did it during the war, queuing up for rations, I would probably have been beaten up where I stood.

Bus queues I'm best at (or should that be worst at?). It doesn't seem to matter how many people are standing there, I always seem to manage to get on in the first half a dozen, and no one has ever protested.

What's the expression? 'It is better to travel than to arrive.' Whichever philosopher came up with that deserves to have a statue erected in his honour in his hometown. To explain why, I will share with you, readers, something that until now has only been in my head. It always seems to give me the screaming abdabs when it happens. It's a bit like my thirty-second law, and I've named it arrival syndrome. It goes a bit like this. Have you ever noticed that when a person on an escalator (and it matters not whether they are going up or coming down) arrives at where the steps disappear into the floor, they step off and immediately embark on a game of statues, standing absolutely still? Do they not think that there just might be someone behind them – or, come to that, twenty-seven people behind them? They know that what they are looking for is on this floor, because they've seen it on the 'store guide', but surely that doesn't mean they have to go up the escalator, stand still at the top and then, stretching their necks like a bad meerkat impression, try to see where the object of their desire is in flagrant disregard of the rest of the world's population coming up the escalator behind them!

People don't just do this on escalators in department stores either. They also do it when they get off a bus. I can't count the times someone has got off a bus in front of me only to stand completely still, whilst a full bus load of passengers has stood behind them in silent queuing disbelief.

Another place they do it is at pelican crossings. When you arrive at a pelican crossing you push the button, as per the instructions, and the 'WAIT' sign flashes up, just as the instructions say it will. Is there anyone out there who can possibly explain to me why what happens next does? The very next person that arrives can surely see that you are standing there. They must be able to – after all, they are actually standing right next to you – and yet without fail they will always, always walk over and push the button a second time. People arriving in twos, deep in conversation, will actually break the conversation just to press the button a second time. Do they not think that I will have already done that? Can they not see that the word 'WAIT' is shining out brightly from the pole, not just on their side of the road but on the other side too, where there are also people standing waiting to cross? And I'm willing to bet they have pushed their button as well. If it's one of those crossings that seem to take for ever to stop the traffic, we move into the next phase, which is that they will go over and press the button again. That's three times, just in case you were losing count, readers. Then another person arrives, sees the two of us standing there and – guess what? Yep, they press it as well. This has always been a source of total mystification to me.

If you want a break from reading, put this book down and go for a walk to your local high street. It's odds-on that you've got a pelican crossing somewhere on it. Go up to it, push the button and see what happens next!

This leads me on to my next subject, and I know that I'm not alone on this one. There I was minding my own business (for once), going up on the escalator in Marks, and about three steps ahead of me was a gent in his sixties. He was muttering away on his mobile phone, seemingly in search of his lost wife. Having got to the top of the escalator he stopped dead in his tracks and he then became the subject of a first-floor pile-up as I and about four others piled into him. Now, I don't put this down entirely to arrival syndrome; to a large extent I put this down to the curse of the mobile phone.

Where do you start when your subject is the greatest must-have gadget of our era? I think the statistic is that for every man, woman and child in Great Britain there is at least one mobile phone. I come from an era where if you told your mate you would see him on Saturday at seven thirty, then at seven thirty he would turn up. If he didn't, then after twenty minutes you'd go home. Then he'd ring on your house phone (it wasn't called a landline then) and say, "Where did you get to?" You'd sort it out and arrange to meet at another time. Mobile phones have changed all of that. As far as I can see, they have only two failings apart from the mobile-phone moan in Chapter 6. Number one is the fact that although the phone is mobile, the person using it doesn't have to be! The number of people who find it impossible to stand still whilst talking on a mobile phone is incredible. Two people standing talking in the street do not walk round each other in ever decreasing circles, looking like they are about to do an impression of an oozlum bird at any minute. So what happens then? What subconscious desire causes people to feel the urge to keep moving whilst clutching a mobile phone? If Sigmund Freud were still alive, he'd have a field day.

The second failing (and this is where I know I'm not alone) is the apparent absolute insane inanity and complete and utter pointlessness of most mobile-phone conversations – especially those you overhear. Nowhere is this more true than on public transport, and on trains in particular. The user seems to think he can't be overheard or that no one is listening, forgetting that he is speaking so loudly and that everybody else is sitting so quietly. It is a jump-out-of-your-skin surprise when suddenly out of nowhere and without warning we are given a window on this person's life away from the 17.04 from London Victoria:

"Hiya. Yeah, it's me. You all right? Yeah, I'm fine. No, I got it. I got it. I got it. Sorry – signal not too good. I said the signal's not too good. Have you been out today? Did you go to the chemist's? The chemist's. Did you go? Yes. And they didn't have one? Oh well, never mind. We'll have a look on Saturday. Saturday, yes. No, I'm on the train now. Oh, we're going through a tunnel. Hello, hello. You still there?"

We now have a break in the conversation as the train passes through the tunnel and the user stares disappointedly at his expensive, momentarily useless, mobile. Upon emergence back into daylight he rings again, but can't get through as his wife (presumably) on the other end is ringing him! After a minute or two of frantically pressing 'redial', contact is re-established. "Hiya. Yeah, it's me. Were you trying to ring me? Ring me. Yes. I did well getting this train – it was a few minutes late so I managed to catch it. Yeah, a couple of minutes. We're just coming in now. Yes, just coming in now, so see you in a minute. Yes. See you in a minute. Yes. OK. Yes. OK. Bye. Bye."

The mobile is then switched off and he gets off the train, which stays long enough at the platform for us to see him meet and kiss his wife (presumably) who was standing waiting for him in the station car park.

What on earth!

What exactly was the point of that conversation? None of it made any sense. He obviously hadn't rung her before, but he decided to ring her less than three minutes before he was due to get off. Could they have not had their chemist/just-made-the-train discussion face-to-face?

Another time, on a trip into London from the South-West, a bloke spent almost an hour on the phone asking his assistant (I'm guessing) to root out some files and spreadsheets ready for him when he arrived. He got off the train with the same cheery "See you in a minute" conversation ender. By the time he'd got off the train everybody in the carriage knew his name, the firm's name, the assistant's name, the assistant's dog's name, the assistant's husband's name, all the kids' names, the school they went to, their teacher, their marks in history, what time the assistant had to leave work on Tuesday next because it was parents' evening and whether it was OK for her to ring the Bangalore office because of the time difference.

Finally, this little moan wouldn't be complete without saying 'hands-free'. Please tell me why someone invented this. It's bad enough people in the street suffering from St Vitus's dance whilst clutching a mobile, but doing it with a 'look, Mum, no hands' approach is annoying and hysterically funny at the same time. I've turned this one to my advantage. I used to get strange looks from people because they thought I was talking to myself (which actually I was, but don't tell anyone), but now thanks to hands-free mobiles I can walk down the street muttering away, laughing out loud, flailing my arms and walking into people without once having to break my train of thought.

The best part of thirty years of my working life have been spent in an office environment, and I have always loved nothing more than the office politics that goes on, all day and every day. One of my favourites is when one of 'the girls' gets up to go to the loo and it starts:

"I see she's wearing that old thing again."

"That's the second time this week, isn't it?"

"Yes, and you can tell she's not washed it – it's filthy round the collar."

"Dirty cow! Hope she's not coming to the Christmas do this year."

"Yeah, she is. She paid the other day."

"Well, I don't want to sit near her. Look out – she's coming back."

The poor girl doesn't have a chance. The best bit is when protagonist one goes to the loo only for the girl to join protagonist two in destroying number one's fashion sense and to discuss whether she uses biological washing powder as well.

I've lost count over the years of how many conversations started with "Did you see blank on the tele last night?" Substitute 'blank' with *EastEnders*, *Corrie*, *Emmerdale*, or some other nondescript programme which I'm sure wasn't in my listings.

I swear that some of them believe soaps are real life!

Of all office discussions, I think my favourite has to be 'What I would do if I won the lottery'. The unshakable beliefs people have regarding what they would do with £15 million are ridiculous in the extreme: from opening llama sanctuaries or funding research into o'nyong-nyong fever to sponsoring nomadic tribesmen. Trust me – over the years I've heard the lot. I would love someone to come out with, just once, "I'm going away on holiday, and never coming back – ever." The conversation usually ends with "I probably wouldn't win; I never put any money on it anyway." No comment at this point, readers, I feel is necessary!

Talking of o'nyong-nyong fever brings us nicely into the world of doctors' waiting rooms. A whole microcosm of human life is here. You check in with the receptionist and after a quick look round you assess which person looks the least ill – perhaps someone who looks like they've got backache rather than someone who keeps scratching at a suspicious-looking rash. Then you squeeze yourself into a seat next to them. What comes next is more listening to the world than watching it. The conversation is usually led by someone who is at least sixty, but usually under eighty, and always encompasses one of three subjects: the government (regardless of who's in power), the cost of everything and (the one that never fails) "Did you know that old Molly's died?" It hasn't got to be Molly, of course, but you can guarantee that they'll know someone who has just recently clog-popped, and all the gory details are shared with us, the disease-ridden throng. Worst of all, thanks to swine flu, you can't bury yourself in one of the newspapers or periodicals, owing to the fact that they don't have them any more – Health & Safety, don't you know.

I don't like popcorn very much. Now, I know what you're thinking, readers: 'He's really gone and lost it this time.' Well, no, I haven't. Why is it that when someone goes to the cinema they have to buy a ginormous tub of the stuff, only half of which then gets eaten? The rest goes sailing through the air in a popcorn blizzard, littering the floor. I have never worked out how the flicks and popcorn got so inextricably linked and how it became a must-have when you go to watch the latest movie. Hardened addicts will actually miss part of the film, dashing out just as it gets to the interesting bit, to feed their habit. Perhaps I should have put this observation on cinema-going into Chapter 5 – but maybe not.

For me, the fascination of watching and nosing what other people are up to has always been that they are often unaware of what they are doing; and, better still, they don't know someone is watching them do it and using it as a source of free entertainment.

I hope you have enjoyed reading about yourselves. I hope you've lost track of how many times you've said to yourself, "Well, he's got that wrong for a start. I've never done that!" Believe me, you do! For those of you that I have converted, I hope you don't burst out laughing the next time you're sitting on a bus or collecting your luggage from the carousel; and, please, I really do not wish you to choke on your prawn cocktail when you suddenly notice how the diner next to you is about to eat their steak-and-ale pie with a spoon!

I hope, too, that I've given you a few laughs along the way whilst telling you all about my adventures into other people's worlds. Those other people, readers, are you; and without you, life, the world and watching it would be an altogether more humdrum experience.

Backword: The World Watching Back

For those of you that have got this far, well done! I admire your stamina, readers. The next time you are on a bus or a train, sitting down for a meal or cheering your favourite team on, look about and see what the gathered throng around you are up to. Doggie people really do say, "C'mon" in a funny, high-pitched, squeaky voice; people really do leap up on a plane when the seat-belt sign goes out; and, believe you me, someone will always, always get up in the middle of a football match for a pie or chips, or both.

Now – and you've got to trust me on this one, readers – having read this book you will surely not only notice what they are up to, but also that no matter what you are doing there will always be some other bugger nosing! Curiosity I can accept; downright nosiness I can't.

I used to think that perhaps it was me and that it didn't happen to other people, but now I'm not so convinced. It always seemed to me that, no matter what I was doing, within two minutes someone would be there to watch me. Nowhere is safe. Nowhere out there is there a hiding place from the nosers. Try it.

Try standing in front of a billboard advertising a forthcoming show at the local theatre and see how long it is before someone arrives, looks over your shoulder and says, "I wouldn't go and see that – not with him in it. I went and saw it last year and it was rubbish."

Try standing at a station reading a railway timetable and see how long it is before someone asks you, "When's the next train to Butterside Down Halt?" (or wherever) or, "Where are the weekend engineering works for the weekend after next?"

And don't, whatever you do, spend too long in a supermarket aisle looking at choccy bickies, because someone will arrive from out of nowhere to tell you how much cheaper the supermarket's own brand is.

They are out there – trust me on this one. They lie in wait, ready to pounce on any unsuspecting soul just minding their own business to confuse them with irrelevant information, passing on worthless knowledge to their poor, defenceless victim. You have to keep your eyes peeled, readers, else they'll have you. You'll have to get in there first. Keep looking over your shoulder and never let your guard drop. Better still, find yourself a position of relative safety from which to watch them. Oh, I have just realised – that's what I've been doing all these years!